# WILLOW RUN FARM

## AN OHIO MEMOIR 1924-1935
### A FLowWOOLF NATURALS SERIES

## MARCELLA WOOLF GRENGA &
## JODY LaRAINE GRENGA

WITH ORIGINAL LINE DRAWINGS BY MARCELLA WOOLF GRENGA
BOOK DESIGN, ORIGINAL GRAPHICS & PHOTOGRAPHS BY JODY LaRAINE GRENGA

### FIRST AMERICAN EDITION
■FLowWOOLF NATURALS, PUBLISHERS

◼PUBLISHED BY FLowWOOLF NATURALS

COPYRIGHT ©2008 BY MARCELLA WOOLF GRENGA & JODY LaRAINE GRENGA

ORIGINAL LINE DRAWINGS, AS ATTRIBUTED (RADIO AND EGG CRATE), COPYRIGHT ©2008 BY MARCELLA WOOLF GRENGA

COVERS, ALL OTHER DESIGNS, GRAPHICS, ILLUSTRATIONS, MAPS AND PHOTOGRAPHS, ATTIBUTED OR UNATTRIBUTED, COPYRIGHT ©2008 BY JODY LaRAINE GRENGA

**WILLOW RUN FARM: AN OHIO MEMOIR 1924-1935
FIRST AMERICAN EDITION**

*Library of Congress Cataloging-in-Publication Data:*
Grenga, Marcella Woolf, 1924-
Grenga, Jody LaRaine, 1956-
    Willow Run Farm: An Ohio Memoir 1924-1935. A FLowWOOLF
    Naturals Series/by Marcella Woolf Grenga and Jody LaRaine
    Grenga; with illustrations by Marcella Woolf Grenga and Jody
    LaRaine Grenga.
    **ISBN:** 978-0-6152-0868-8   (paperback)
    1. Memoir-- Non-Fiction. 2. The Great Depression-- Non-
Fiction. 3. Subsistence Farming-- Non-Fiction.    4.   Ohio-- Non-
Fiction. 5. Northeast Ohio. 6. Autobiography. I. Grenga, Jody LaRaine

QUESTIONS REGARDING CONTENT SHOULD BE ADDRESSED TO:
**FLowWOOLF@SWBELL.NET**

QUESTIONS REGARDING BOOK ORDERS SHOULD BE ADDRESSED TO:
**HTTP://WWW.LULU.COM/CONTENT/2429530**

*Printed in the United States of America*
*Book design, production and page layout by* Jody LaRaine Grenga

# DEDICATION.

*t*O the memory of my mother, my father and my siblings Florence, Doris, Delmus and Homer. For my sister, Elaine.

# PRIOR PUBLICATIONS.

JODY LaRAINE GRENGA, "Sales Force: Selling Tactics sWIPED from the Army," a FLowWOOLF Naturals Series, published by FLowWOOLF Naturals, ©2007

JODY LaRAINE GRENGA, manuscript and graphics for the Biography of Florence Scovel Shinn, in "The Writings of Florence Scovel Shinn," DeVorss Publishers, ©1996

# CONTENTS.

# Contents.

# CONTENTS.

Figure 1: MAP of BERLIN CENTER, MAHONING COUNTY,
STATE of OHIO, UNITED STATES of AMERICA. By J. GRENGA.

## ACKNOWLEDGEMENTS.

**f**RUITFUL thanks to folks everywhere revitalizing sustainable agriculture. The authors feel privileged to live in Austin, Texas, hometown of Barton Springs Pool and Whole Foods Market. Bushels of thanks to Central Market and Sun Harvest Farms.

**C**ORNUCOPIC thanks to the Sunset Valley Farmers Market, an award-winning enterprise promoting organic, locally grown, <u>seasonal</u> produce. Flavory thanks to market anchor Jackie Pomrenke, Flintrock Farms, Kingsbury, Texas-- for yard eggs (orange yolks), fragrant strawberries and fire-engine-red tomatoes; beefy thanks to the Sams family, Full Quiver Farm, Kemp, Texas, especially Mike for insights on Jersey bulls; and to all others at the Sunset Valley Farmers Market.

## ACKNOWLEDGEMENTS.

**G**ENEROUS slices of "thank-you" pie to my sister, Martha Elaine Woolf Tomkinson, *encourageur*; to Beverly Lockhart, for her photographs of née-Mill Creek schoolhouse; to Brenda Reynolds, for taking time to record the memoirs of my father, Byron, and my sister, Florence (Brenda's mother); ambrosial thanks to Kathy Strittmatter, for her discerning taste regards book design and "Nourishing Traditions" food experiments; sweet thanks to Stacy L. Shoup, Spangler Candy Company, Bryan, Ohio; Archivist Arlene May, Sears Holdings Historical Archives, Hoffman Estates, Illinois; Pamela Speis and Priscilla Sutton, Archives, Mahoning Valley Historical Society, Youngstown, Ohio; judicious thanks to Joel White, Esquire, Austin, Texas, for his guidance; a jamboree of thanks to Alyssa Carpenter for giving Jody a clutch of vintage glass jars.

**A** SMÖRGÅS*BIRD* of thanks to Torrey the *Catalogeur*, for some*rassaulting* over the keyboard gingerly (and quite entertainingly), and to the Royal *Surveyeur*, Edison "Timmers" Hemmingway.

--MG, JLG

# Author's Foreword.

*"Why be difficult*
*when with a little more effort*
*you could be Impossible?"*

NOW realize that my parents' decision to venture into poultry farming around 1930 saved my family from the clutches of the Great Depression. Only when giving this manuscript a final polish, was I struck by the realization that Willow Run Farm spared us from oblivion. Countless other families were overwhelmed, then succumbed, lost their homes and lost everything.

Without such a farm-- my dad might have been forced to abandon our farm or to have ordered my older brother or sister to leave home. At the depth of the Depression, more than four million Americans— women and men alike— took to the rails, including 250,000 teenagers. These homeless wayfarers were seeking food and shelter—above all, work.

In 1920, America was officially recognized as an urban nation when the city-dwelling population rose to 50 percent. By 1930, that figure jumped to nearly 70 percent, leaving fewer Americans to tend farms. I record these memoirs as a tribute to my parents, who kept our farm throughout the Depression. We were among the 30 percent of folk who avoided flocking in droves to cities already flooded with millions of other Americans and immigrants. All told, from 1929 to 1932, some 400,000 farmers lost their land.

Willow Run Farm survived.

*I*N 2003, we began to write. I had just come off a World Cruise that April. My daughter, Jody, had long encouraged me to write my memoirs. *It was time.* Jody sat at a laptop in her breakfast room. I stood behind her. While she typed, I dictated snippets. I started off talking about my dad. We saved the project as "Willow Run" in the computer, 'though I casually referred to our project as my *"Momoirs."*

*"Why do I have to dictate this?"* I thought, after a few sessions. *"I can sit at home and type this myself."* So I did. Discarding the piece on my dad, I started from scratch. Over a period of several days, I typed 26 pages on my own computer, using Microsoft Word as my word-processing program.

Alas! All for naught. Reluctantly, I must admit to my word-processing shortcomings. I "lost" all 26 pages a few days into the "Run." In one minute! I don't know exactly how— but I deleted my manuscript.

My co-author figures it this way: When I went to close Word one day, an icon likely popped up:

**DO YOU WANT TO SAVE THE CHANGES TO "WILLOW RUN"?**

By reflex, I clicked **YES** --had I looked, I would have seen the screen only was displaying a half-dozen words. In hindsight, I must have highlighted the document inadvertently (most of its 26 pages) then clicked **ENTER**, handily erasing the bulk of my document. Thus, clicking that **YES** saved the erasure. Permanently.

The six words that were not deleted haunted us for months. All that remained of my nascent book was a cryptic shred, something like: "*Willow Run Farm was not always the...*" Jody methodically scoured the innards of my computer and every floppy disc we owned, but no secret memory-cache of my manuscript surfaced.

I swallowed my pride in 2005. Flo, my oldest sister, died at age 95 that October. Nostalgia moved me to begin *a third time.* I was determined to rebuild those 26 cheeky pages. I couldn't bring myself to do it earlier-- too humiliated by my gaffe.

Jody pointed out that the manuscript seemed to exist in my mind like an unbroken thread. This simile compelled me to complete this account of my early years. It was the least I could do out of appreciation for my mother and my family. Resolved, I typed for three or four hours a day for several weeks. The words poured out of me, nearly identical to those I had inadvertently zapped. My memories are vivid. I typed as fast as I could.

I reconstructed those d*mn 26 pages from memory.

Meanwhile, in May 2004, I had been declared legally blind. I was embarrassed-- in such good health, to think a condition like macular degeneration had caught up with me! As I began reconstructing my manuscript, I noticed a difference between my visual acuity regarding the computer screen in 2003 versus 2005. I became unable to perform spelling checks accurately. My visual impairment was affecting my ability to read what I had typed-- editing flew out the window—even more frustrating because I am a competent typist. I just kept typing— unconcerned about paragraphing and spacing-- nonplussed at my inability to punctuate and tab, to correct grammar and spelling.

I simply stuck with my original intent: finish it.

I cautiously clicked the **SAVE** icon after each paragraph. Religiously! Har har.

I worked diligently for six weeks. Those 26 *blankety-blank* pages were rebuilt and by the close of 2005 I had expanded my memoirs to 92 single-spaced pages. This version (this saved version) languished in my computer another 16 months.

In April 2007, began Round IV. Jody began editing the 92-page document at my house. She separated the text into a dozen or so categories, e.g.: "The Garden," "The School," "The House." She combed the manuscript to extract and organize material pertinent to each category. Her questions to me helped flesh out the bones.

"What color hair?" Jody asked. "What flavor pie?" "What kind of radio?"

The project got set aside again.

December 30, 2007, we got serious. Time to take this baby to the bank. Jody had finished editing her first book and we both had the time to begin anew. Each morning at 9:40, I walked eight-tenths of a mile to my bus stop. Jody met me at her bus stop. We walked another seven-tenths of a mile together, to her house. (Using public transportation to get around augments a sense of independence from my visual condition.)

We spent January through June working a minimum of five hours a day, six days a week-- adding, deleting, editing, illustrating. I dictated once again while Jody typed. Alas, we had come full circle in this fifth, final and successful attempt. I doodled on loose-leaf paper or conjured up ways to keep the cat from walking on the keyboard while Jody she cut and pasted in Word or switched my brilliant prose from passive to active voice. At one point, we were curious as to how many verb constructions contained the word "would"—we stopped counting at 240 and trimmed out about 213 of those. We deliberated the merits of typing an "a" versus using a "the." Who knew we had it in us! From memory, I drew farm and household implements from the 1930's. We sketched floor plans of the old farmhouse, garden and a diagram of the farmstead. For black and white drawings, I used a thick Sharpie marker to see well enough what I was drawing. Jody showed me how to thicken the lines so they photographed nicely.

"Did we get anything <u>done</u> today?" one of us asked at the end of each session.

"I think we got a <u>lot</u> done today, don't you?" the other answered— a veritable mutual admiration society.

I feel a great sense of accomplishment. I had the humility to start my project anew (five times) and see it to fruition. In 2005, I replicated those infamous 26 pages. In 2008, with Jody's writing and interviewing skills (interviewing <u>me</u>) -- together we doubled the length of my manuscript and managed to eke out this book.

The pure magic of the computer awes me— imagine pecking away at a typewriter! The Internet has almost everything: inexhaustible reference material at the fingertips; an online thesaurus (¿What's the plural of "thesaurus"?!) and dictionaries for English... and other foreign languages; photos of old gadgets. The technology to snap a photo and-- in the *blink of an iris* (the iris of a digital camera) — insert it instantly into our text added a novel dimension to the project. Jody has an exceptional ability to find anything on the Internet in three minutes (or less); to organize— whether building a chapter outline or restructuring a paragraph; to copy, clip, cut, paste, reverse, save, adhere to "Strunk & White" (more...or less); to provide background material; to transform everyday objects digitally into *objets d'art*. I am learning these *magics* as my eyesight improves. Had I been typing my memoirs 50 years ago on a Corona portable typewriter—

it would have taken me 50 years to write it!    I'd be finishing it up just about now!

These are *my* memoirs, told largely from the perspective of a 7-year-old child. I have laid down my memories and we have reconstructed conversation with best effort.  This book, Volume I of a trilogy, is divided into four parts:  My Family, The House, Mill Creek School Years and Victual Rituals.    These four parts are subdivided into chapters.   Each chapter includes a panoramic-view narrative (*àla* home movies); photographs of actual family artifacts (or models thereof); and a quip my family bandied about.  Each chapter also is accompanied by a "Vignette," a literary device my co-author invented to highlight precious snapshots: stand-alone freeze-frames ranging from barefoot summer antics to harsh realities of life on our Depression-era farm.

Writing about food in "Willow Run" (which was so often I was given to homesickness), describing buttered loaves of bread hot out of the oven, blackberry pie, ham and eggs, golden-fried mush, baked custard— made me sentimental for the taste of my mother's cooking. It makes me want to cry, to think of it now.

# Co-Author's Preface.

*"...I'VE BEEN SITTING HERE TYPING THE PAST NINETY MINUTES FOR THREE HOURS."*

--JLG

URING the five years I've been honored to assist with this project, I evolved from a casual strolling sampler at our local Farmers Market to an employee. Among the 122+ seasonal and/or year-'round vendors (selling crafts, fresh produce and prepared food), fresh-produce stalls attract the longest queues. To paraphrase my Market pal, Kathy: "Folks are paying good money nowadays at the Farmers Market to replicate the way the Woolf family ate (which was cheaply) on their farm during the Depression." Globally (not only in Austin), cravings are intensifying for fresh, locally grown, natural and seasonal food such as we write about herein. People are clamoring for real food.

During the decade sandwiched by this book, a war was long smoldering. This timeframe was a skull-and-cross*roads* of growing agribusiness conglomerates crossing the American consumer. Cleveland dentist Weston A. Price was practicing 60 miles from Willow Run Farm, soon to investigate why "primitive" peoples had remarkably healthier dentition (largely from including lacto-fermented food, e.g., kefir, in their diets) than Americans. Giant corporations tapped the hottest, newest fab-advertising medium ever invented: *Radios* were priced cheaply— deliberately— to lure consumers into spending "more on less." Campaigns mounted to shove *myth*-information down a consumer's throat: that oleomargarine was butter than better (oops!); that saccharine was superior to sugar; that white bread was more nutritious than whole-grain; that skim (or powdered or pasteurized) milk was better than raw, whole, unpasteurized, unhomogenized milk; that Crisco and other hydrogenated vegetable oils were better than pig-fat lard. Indeed, Procter & Gamble (maker of Ivory soap and Crisco) sponsored so many radio programs during this period-- the shows were dubbed "soap operas."

Improvements in food preservation technology turned up the heat, convincing consumers that frozen and canned foods were cheaper and more nutritious (not to mention, simpler to prepare) than fresh foods. Americans were told that candy was nutritious "energy food!" The following products were introduced, invented, isolated, patented or produced in the year indicated:

- **1771:** FIRST SYNTHETIC DYE (PICRIC ACID, FROM INDIGO)
- **1802:** POWDERED MILK
- **1855:** EARLIEST FORM OF PLASTIC
- **1858:** VANILLIN (ARTIFICIAL VANILLA)
- **1873:** OLEOMARGARINE BECAME AVAILABLE IN AMERICA
- **1878:** SACCHARIN (ARTIFICIAL SUGAR)
- **1898:** CORN OIL
- **1902:** HYDROGENATED VEGETABLE OIL (IMPLICATED IN MACULAR DEGENERATION & OTHER CONDITIONS)
- **1911:** CRISCO (FROM "<u>CRYS</u>TALLIZED <u>CO</u>TTONSEED OIL")
- **1922:** FROZEN FOOD (COMMERCIALLY AVAILABLE)
- **1965:** ASPARTAME (NUTRASWEET)
- **1967:** COOL WHIP

Since 2005, I have experimented with recipes in "Nourishing Traditions," a cookbook incorporating Dr. Price's findings. I have made my own butter, cultured buttermilk, kefir (all from raw, fresh farm milk); kombucha (tea); lacto-fermented Korean sauerkraut (kim chee); baked custard; raw-cure (low temperature) dried fruits and beef jerky. From the Farmers Market, I enjoy free-range eggs, no-nitrate bacon, decent tomatoes, cucumbers, beets, strawberries, pecans, Swiss chard. Attempting to replicate some of the dishes my grandma Woolf served in Marcella's childhood—I find gratifying.

Co-authoring "Willow Run Farm" has been a fascinating journey. I am conversant now on a variety of new topics: foremost, the history of toilet paper; the curious fact that many devices, products and tools were implemented (widely) more than 50 years after their invention; Frank Lloyd Wright's post-1908 designs for Sears, Roebuck mail-order homes; perfection of the Holstein-Friesian cattle breed in The Netherlands; the horrific connection between oil-paint pigments (e.g., Paris Green), Monet's blindness and Van Gogh's insanity; early chocolate bars and Dum-Dum suckers; and why rhubarb is planted along the edge of a garden (it comes up year after year, so must be protected from getting trampled).

I have strived to preserve the flavor of speech from northeast Ohio, e.g., "rid up" for "clean;" "barb" wire; and "foot" used in dimensions; and to convey the Woolf family's wit via quips (chapter headers) and wordplay.

Marcella's wit and intelligence is borne out in these pages. Perhaps not so evident is her determination, devotion, discipline and dedication. She opened herself up to finding a way to finishing this manuscript after being diagnosed as legally blind and did just that. She patiently sat to my right while I typed. Marcella has a near-photographic ability that lets her memorize events and large blocks of text. Marcella's sense of humor and easy-going nature let this project be a consummate learning experience and consummate joy.

--JODY LaRAINE GRENGA
AUSTIN, TEXAS

# VIGNETTE: SUCKER PUNCH.

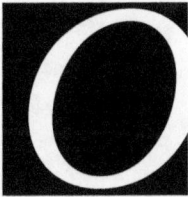

O N ANOTHER OCCASION, DODIE, ELAINE, HOMER AND I CAME DOWN WITH THE MEASLES IN MAY. IT WAS HOT UPSTAIRS. THE BEDROOM, EVEN WITH ALL THE WINDOWS IN THE HOUSE OPEN, WAS STIFLING. FLO HAD HER 20-YEAR-OLD PAL, MARTHA STEWART (NOT THE MARTHA STEWART) HELPING OUT. MARTHA SPONGE-BATHED US WITH COLD WASHCLOTHS AND BROUGHT US WATER TO SIP. MARTHA AIDED US WHEN WE NEEDED TO RELIEVE OURSELVES IN THE BUCKET AND RELIEVED MOTHER TO ATTEND TO THE DOMESTIC DUTIES.

A GROCERY TRUCK CAME BY THREE TIMES A WEEK. WE KIDS BOUGHT PENNY SUCKERS. WE WERE ALWAYS ON THE LOOKOUT, HOPING TO FIND A RARE "PROMOTIONAL" WOUND AROUND THE STICK, HIDDEN UNDER THE WRAPPER. THIS PIECE OF PAPER ANNOUNCED THAT THE RECIPIENT HAD WON A "SUPER DUM-DUM" FREE. REGULAR DUM-DUM LOLLIPOPS, INTRODUCED IN THAT MOST WONDERFUL YEAR (1924) WERE ROUND, ABOUT THE SIZE OF A QUARTER. THEY HAD A LITTLE RIDGE AROUND THE TOP. THE SUPER DUM-DUM WAS DISC-SHAPED, FOUR INCHES ACROSS (FROM WEST TO EAST) AND A HALF-INCH THICK. I GAVE MY COUPON TO THE DRIVER TO REDEEM. *"BRING ME A GREEN ONE!"* I SAID. MEANWHILE, WE CAME DOWN WITH THE MEASELS. THE GROCERY MAN RETURNED LATER WITH MY PRIZE. HE GAVE IT TO MOTHER FOR SAFEKEEPING. SHE INNOCENTLY LAID IT ON OUR DRESSER, PERHAPS TO EGG-ON MY RECOVERY. WHICH MAKES IT ALL THE MORE TRAGIC. IN THE COURSE OF HELPING OUT, MARTHA SPOTTED MY PRIZE. IT ATE AT HER TO SEE IT LYING THERE TEASINGLY. IN A BRASH MANEUVER, SHE BROUGHT A HAMMER UPSTAIRS WITH MALICE AFORETHOUGHT. THAT SAUCY TART SMASHED MY HUGE SUCKER INTO BITE-SIZED PIECES WITH THE HAMMER.

"THAT'S MARCELLA'S!" FLO SAID, AGHAST-- A CAUTION TOO LATE.

"OH, THAT'S OK...!" MARTHA SAID. "...SHE'S TOO SICK TO EAT IT ANYWAY!" WE YOUNGSTERS ALL WATCHED DUM(B)STRUCK AS MARTHA DEVOURED MY SUPER DUM-DUM AT LEISURE. SHE HAD TAKEN IT UPON HERSELF TO EAT MY TREASURE. WE WERE TOO SICK TO SQUEAK OUT A PROTEST OR GET UP AND THROTTLE HER. BUT WE WANTED TO. THE BRAZEN ACT. I CAN'T SAY IF FLO PARTICIPATED IN THIS SAVAGERY. IF SHE DID I'LL FORGIVE HER. BUT MARTHA STEWART— SHE GOT HER COMEUPPANCE LATER. ISN'T THAT FUNNY, I CAN STILL SEE THE WAY SHE CRACKED MY DUM-DUM UP TO EAT IN FRONT OF US. ALAS, THIS PROVED THE ONLY TIME I WON A SUPER DUM-DUM IN MY LIFE.          --C. 1930

# INTRODUCTION.

*I*RONICALLY the little creek that gave our farm its name did not even have a name of its own. We just knew it as "the crick." It meandered along the south boundary of our farm. The remains of a mill trace laid out in the 1800's ran from below the barn, although its gristmill had since washed away in a flash flood, or otherwise had met its demise long before our time.

The small feathery trees that lined the creek on its north bank inspired my father to call our homestead "Willow Run Farm."

Today, the house, more than 100 years old, still stands. Ownership has passed from my family, the Woolfs. The white-frame structure faces State Route 534 just south of its intersection with Western Reserve Road. The nearest town is Berlin Center, two and a half miles north of the house. This stretch of "534" was formally known as "South Pricetown Road."

This corner of northeast Ohio is rich in history. It was Johnny Appleseed's domain. It was a parcel carved out of Connecticut Land Company holdings, a tract that originally extended from sea-to-sea. It originated at the Atlantic Ocean and mapped-out through Indiana and Illinois to the Pacific Ocean at California. Hence they named it, eponymously, the "Western Reserve." A glance at 18th-century maps reveals the breadth of the State of Connecticut at the time— about as tall as today but as a phenomenally-long strip. Tracing one's index finger from Connecticut, through its "Reserve to the West," curiously reveals an east-to-west straight line right through Berlin Center, Mahoning County, Ohio (a realization most astounding and *breadth*-taking).

Willow Run Farm was carved out of section "5" in northwest Goshen Township. Western Reserve Road has several distinctions: it marked the northern boundary line of our farmstead; it marked Goshen Township's boundary with Berlin Township to the north; on a larger scale, and historically-- it formed the <u>southern</u> boundary of the Connecticut Western Reserve as it extended through what became Mahoning County. Thus, from the perspective of Willow Run Farm, Western Reserve Road ran east nearly to the Pennsylvania border. (One might argue that Western Reserve Road to the east came westward into our sector of Ohio <u>from</u> Pennsylvania, rather.)

The house was built in 1903. The roof is a work of art, tiled with elegant light gray, octagonally-shaped slate shingles. These lent a most distinguished look to our house. The date was written across the roof using darker slate tiles "east" of the dormer:

## 1903

This well-built two-story farmhouse provided solid comfort for our family of eight during the thin years of the Depression. We were poor but we always had enough to eat. A reader might be tempted to come away from this memoir with the conviction that we were fairly well off. Yet, there was never enough cash for any frivolities or extravagances, only the basics. My thesis stands: That all eight of us Woolfs pitching in to grow our own food kept us on the survival side of a razor-thin line separating us from the other side: starvation.

Among the multitude of literary accounts regarding the Depression, the most famous is John Steinbeck's "The Grapes of Wrath," his 1939 masterpiece that won both the Pulitzer Prize and the Nobel Prize.

*b*YRON Eli Woolf, my father, had a grade-school education. His younger brothers, Emerson Clyde and Fred Guy, were bestowed the privilege of graduating from college. Emerson earned a law degree and I do not know what Fred *colleged* in. My grandfather Woolf pulled Byron (but not Byron's two brothers or sister, Mary) out of school periodically to help with planting and harvesting and general farm chores. On the other hand, Emerson and Fred did forge on to finish high school and college.

Byron never completed seventh grade.

My dad resented this injustice all his life.

"They got to go to college," he often said, "and I didn't." He said it so many times it seemed obvious he was bitter. Emerson visited us a couple times a month-- he brought Dad good, serviceable second-hand suits of fine clothes. As an attorney, Emerson kept up with men's fashion. As adults, the brothers had a close relationship and Byron was not outwardly raw. Bryon was shrewd, industrious, fair and honest— then again, such honesty might have rendered him fit for other than lawyering. But who is to say my dad could not have succeeded in college himself? He had the mind of an inventor and engineer.

As a child, I recall visiting my dad's parents. My grandfather, Howard, treated Dad as an equal and seemed to appreciate Dad's intellect and wit. My grandpa Woolf was a great kidder also, it wasn't my dad alone. Therefore the nearly-inexcusable discrepancy in the Woolf siblings' education was perhaps an unfortunate matter of birth order, as it fell that Byron was born the eldest son.

*b*LANCHE Othel Cline, my mother, told me once that she only went through fifth grade. Any chance she might have had to graduate from high school was cut short. Byron at age 23 was forcibly persuaded to marry Blanche when she was days from delivering their first child in 1910.

Blanche was a few months shy of 16 at the time.

She was pleasant and sweet natured and hard working. She didn't let things get under her skin.

She was a gentle soul. Blanche recognized her responsibility of tending to her family and that was her pursuit in life. And she did it well. She never appeared to have been bitter about having to get married.

The point is, Blanche never complained, that's all. She seemed to have let it go.

My eldest sibling, Florence, played a big role in my growing up years. Clearly her childhood was abbreviated at age 6 with the birth of a sibling, Delmus, in 1916. Like Byron and Blanche, Flo probably didn't have much of a "childhood" either. My parents expected Flo to assume some mothering duties toward her new brother. Flo was called upon to mother my two older sisters, me and our younger brother in succession.

Flo was determined to get an education. Like her uncles Emerson and Fred before her, achieving a college education was rare among rural Americans then. Her goal in life was to teach school and that she did.

f LORENCE died in her sleep while visiting Marcellus, New York in 2005. The irony strikes home. Flo claimed she named me. "Marcella" is the feminine version of the Latin, *Marcellus*-- meaning "little Marcus."

The parcel of land where Flo was buried (Lumberton Cemetery) and her homestead ("Brooke Lawnne," where she lived 64 years) were poignantly carved out of our land at Willow Run Farm. As kids, we picked fruit near the fence of that cemetery for Mother's plum preserves and plum pies.

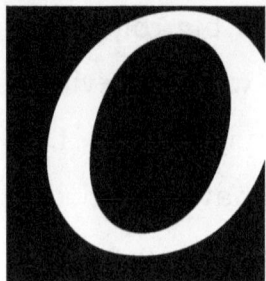

**O**NE of my fondest childhood memories is of the aroma of food wafting from the kitchen into every corner of the house-- apple pies or baked custard or blackberry cobbler or baking bread; bacon and ham or sausage sizzling in an iron skillet with potatoes— all sent tantalizing beckons from the stove.

I recollect a warm, loving family life although my family did not outwardly demonstrate gestures of affection. Discipline, when it came, was swift and harsh.

Outside, our house was never painted anything but white. Inside, it was spacious-- eight rooms and a full basement. Judged according to the standards of the time, our house was well appointed-- although during my entire childhood we used an outhouse. We had but one indoor bathroom with a tub and a sink.

We had, that is, no indoor toilet.

Volume I of this trilogy of memoirs begins with 1924, the year of my birth, through completion in 1935 of my elementary education in a one-room school. "Willow Run Farm" is a chronicle of my family's gritty determination to adapt successfully to the Depression. Volume II will encompass the years 1936 through my highschool graduation in 1941. Volume III will cover my training as a registered nurse during World War II.

# MY IMMEDIATE FAMILY.

# VIGNETTE:
## TOP 10 GIRLS' NAMES, 1924.

MOST POPULAR GIRLS' NAMES OF 1924. "MARCELLA" ISN'T IN THE TOP 10 (OR THE TOP 100).

- *M*ARY
- *D*OROTHY
- *H*ELEN
- *B*ETTY
- *M*ARGARET
- *R*UTH
- *V*IRGINIA
- *M*ILDRED
- *D*ORIS
- *F*RANCES

# CHAPTER 1:
## THE BREAKFAST.

*"SHOULD A BOOK ABOUT A CHICKEN FARM WIN A PULLET-ZER PRIZE?"*

--JLG

ER morning ritual includes rising at 6. She hurriedly dresses to ward off the cold. She goes downstairs to light the wood stove. She uses coal. It is cheaper than buying wood. Three or four scoops from the coal scuttle sitting next to the stove do nicely. She opens the forward right burner plate and dumps in the coal. One swift swipe with a "strike anywhere" match and some kindling-- soon Mother has a contained blaze going in the firebox. (Perhaps she formulated her plan for breakfast on the way down the steps.)

"Shall I make oatmeal with the ham or just eggs and fried potatoes," she might have mused. "Or shall we have mush this morning?"

She settles on cornmeal mush and fried eggs and forgets about the oatmeal and fried potatoes. This will make a hearty meal.

Having decided on the fare, she sets to slicing the ham. The night before, she had asked Dad to bring up some ham from the basement when he was down there nailing a nail in the wall. She met him halfway on the cellar steps to hand him the butcher knife. He cut off a substantial chunk. He was tall enough and the ceiling low enough that he merely had to reach up to the ham hanging on the joist and hack off a portion of the ham hanging there, air-curing. The ham was more than a foot in all dimensions. The piece he cut off was maybe 6 by 4 by 3 or so inches. Dad might have "rubbed some salt into the wound" he left, by taking a handful of curing salts from the other side of the ham and smearing it onto the fresh cut. Mother stored this piece of ham overnight on top of the stove with a coarse cloth draped over it.

APPARENTLY THE HAM DID NOT SPOIL OVERNIGHT— NO ONE GOT *KLEPTOMAINIA*. GOSH, HOW UNSANITARY! THE ONLY POSSIBLE SEQUELA IS THAT THE HAM COULD HAVE TURNED GAN*GREEN*OUS. (REMEMBER, I'M STILL HERE AFTER ±80 YEARS.)

Mother takes down two large cast-iron skillets from hooks hanging over the stove. She places the pans atop the pair of front burners to warm up as the stove warms. While the skillets heat, she cuts the ham. The slices are nearly a fourth-inch thick. She has to slice the ham at the stove. (Mother doesn't have any counter space. Who knows if Mother had a cutting board or not. I don't think Dad ever made her one. I don't recall a cutting board.)

Remember, Flo isn't present. She was 20 when I was 6. She is at Kent Normal School but the other five children are at home.

From experience, Mother knows when the skillets are hot enough by touching the handles. She flips a glob of lard into each pan. Soon, upstairs, still abed, I smell pig fat frying. White and glistening and slippery, it sizzles and slides in the pan as it melts.

The day before, Mother had made cornmeal mush. She boiled corn meal in salted water until it thickened. She poured the mixture into pre-greased bread loaf tins to gel overnight. Now she is ready to slice the solidified mush.  She pops it out of the pan.  Mother slices it deftly. Half-inch thick slabs of bright yellow cornmeal mush go into the liquid, bubbling pig fat.

Crumbs of cornmeal mush dance in the hot skillet. For a second, Mother watches them with fascination yet is careful to avoid being spattered with hot grease. Meanwhile, sliced ham and eggs are frying in the other iron skillet.  All of us like our eggs over hard, so she cracks the yolk on the eggs and turns them over to fry evenly.

Mother lifts her blue-and-white speckled and quite beat-up graniteware coffee pot.  She fills it from the "spicket" [spigot] at the sink.  She spoons ground coffee into the basket, replaces the lid and lets the brew come to a boil.  By this time the acrid smell of coffee is also tickling my nose.  Mother is ready to finalize breakfast. She comes to the upstairs doorway.

"Breakfast will be ready in a few minutes!" she says, calling to us from the bottom of the stairs, genteelly.

Of course we don't have to wash up or anything. And of course she doesn't have to call us twice.  There was no bathroom upstairs.  We merely have to jump into our clothes and go down.

Mother is a short-order cook.  She has to turn over the mush.  She has to turn over the eggs.  Turn over the ham.  She has to pour milk into our glasses.  Fill the coffee cups. Replenish the butter. At times, we kids clumsily turn over our glasses filled with milk.

Mom's mush turns out perfectly. It is so good, its dark- browned, crispy surface contradicting a creamy, hot interior. Mother moves the skillets to the side to avoid scorching the meal while keeping the delectables warm. She serves the first round. Meanwhile, she hastens to place seven plates on the table, along with forks, knives, glasses and cups-- we kids will slurp milk and Mother and Dad will sip their coffee.

We don't have paper napkins.

The coffee is boiling and ready for pouring. All five at-home kids have scrambled downstairs with Dad. Now we are sitting at the table staring longingly at bread and farm butter and blackberry jam and Aunt Jemima "sirp" and our white, empty plates. Patience and politeness prevail for now. Mother takes the finished mush out of the skillet and stacks it on a platter. She slices more mush and puts it in the skillet for another go-'round and slides the skillet back atop the burner. A little more lard gets plopped in. As Mother approaches the breakfast table, we know better than to lunge into the bread and butter and jam. (Oh! my gosh. I'm going out of my mind with the thought of everyone seated at the table antsily awaiting this feast.) Mother places the platters of mush and ham and eggs on the table and returns to her frying.

I grow tempted to pick up a loose morsel of mush, eye-balling me from the big white platter. But I think better of it. We pass the food around family style.

"Stop it!" Martha Elaine says abruptly, hissing at Dodie. Elaine squirms in her chair. "Stop it!" she repeats. Dodie smirks.

"What's goin' on?" Dad asks, without looking up from his plate.

"She kicked my chair," Elaine says.

"Did not."

"Did too, ya dummy!"

"Did not," Dodie says.

"Elaine! Quit provoking her," Mother says from the stove.

"Don't tell me, Doris," Dad says. "You kicked her on purpose accident'ly."

Dodie puts her head down almost to her plate and grins widely. She has won this round.

Elaine is in tears but says no more. She cries at the unfairness of it all.

Mother brings two cups of coffee to the table. Her brown-and-white ceramic cream pitcher is handy and full. Mother and Dad cherish their coffee in the morning.

Mother is not able to sit down yet with the family. She prepares Dad's dinner bucket. She has to put coffee in a Thermos for him, make one or two sandwiches and chuck in a piece of pie she has saved from the night before. (Perhaps it had been sitting out on the stove next to the ham.) The pie she wraps in "wax" paper (*and a plastic fork to eat it with*-- just kidding). With Dad's dinner pail packed, she sits down with us to taste her coffee. She still isn't able to eat her breakfast because more mush is frying and she has to baby Homer.

Mother stirs her cup of half cream and half coffee, while we eat like no one is looking. With Mother's irresistible food on the table, our manners are no fit for an audience with Queen Mary. No polished English— no pinkie-crooking while *glurping* glasses of milk.

We don't own a toaster. Mother's efforts to toast fresh white bread on the oven racks resulted in freshly blackened bread, always. Mother tried to scrape the burned layer off the bread a time or two and decided it was not worth the bother. We are equally tickled to devour her homemade bread simply with a smear of her dandelion-yellow butter.

"Clean up your plate, Homer..." Mother says softly. "...the children in <u>China</u> are starving." Homer looks at her. He is perplexed. At age 4, he has no more idea where China is than how to roof a corn crib. The rest of us don't have to be told to clean up our plates because we do clean up our plates. A tear-off of Mother's fresh bread serves nicely to sop up a last pool of syrup and mop a plate dry.

When everyone is finished eating, Doris and Elaine clear the table of dirty dishes and put them in the sink. Elaine accidentally bumps Dodie on purpose with a plate. The two of them then make sandwiches for our school lunches. They butter the hand-sliced bread and use leftover slices of ham and extra fried eggs, if any. (This will taste luxurious later at school during recess.)

Doris wraps the sandwiches in newspaper, preferably one Dad has already read. We wash our hands, comb our hair, put on our coats and hats and boots. It is getting on about 7:30 now and we have to think about trudging a mile to school. Delmus is 14 and doesn't walk with us to Mill Creek School. He waits for the bus on the Goshen High School run.

Dad lingers a few minutes over his hot coffee.

"I must go," he says, and pushes back his chair. He puts on his jacket and hat. He always wore a Fedora. He takes up his dinner bucket and heads out the door for his car. (This is winter we're talking about because the kids have jackets and boots on. We kept the screen door tethered back, so Mother didn't need to warn us against slamming it. I'd like to think we gave Mother a peck on the cheek as we laid out our goodbyes. Perhaps not.)

Mother has a minute to relax as the last one trips out the back door.

She had set aside her breakfast platter of ham, mush and eggs. She always makes sure we get fed, with enough left over for lunches, with everybody ready and off to a clean start before she eats. By then her meal is cold. Homer stays home. He keeps Mother company as she finishes her breakfast.

Homer got babied a lot. Mother really babied him.

With us out of her hair, Mother washes and dries the dishes. Perhaps it is a Monday and she will start the wash-- Monday is washday. Or if it is Tuesday, she will begin her ironing...

# VIGNETTE: THE HAY MOW.

W E ALSO SPENT A LOT OF TIME UP AT THE BARNYARD CONVERSING WITH THE ANIMALS AND PETTING THEM. WE PLAYED IN THE BARN, IN THE HAY MOW ("MOW" RHYMES WITH "HOW") AND STRAW MOW AND JUMPED FROM THE HIGH WOODEN SUPPORT BEAMS INTO THE PILES OF STRAW. WE WERE NOT SUPPOSED TO DO THAT BECAUSE IT MATTED THE STRAW, RENDERING IT USELESS. ON ONE OCCASION I JUMPED ONTO A ROLL OF BARB WIRE WHICH WAS SECRETED IN THE STRAW. I SUFFERED MULTIPLE BARBED PUNCTURE MARKS AND LACERATIONS ON BOTH LEGS. MOTHER TO THE RESCUE-- ALONG WITH BEING A HOUSEKEEPER SHE WAS A PRACTICAL NURSE. BLESS HER.

I STILL CARRY SCARS ON THE SIDE OF MY RIGHT LEG FROM THIS INDISCRETION.

--C. 1934

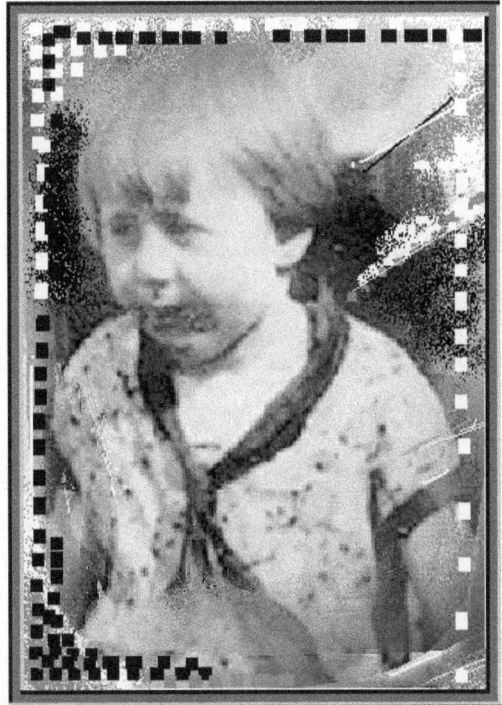

# CHAPTER 2:
## I AM BORNDED.

*"WAS I A FRUIT OF MY MOTHER'S LABOR?"*

**m**Y parents, sisters and brother awaited my birth. I wonder what kind of a splash I made or was it old hat by then. Mother wanted to get this over with (surely), having endured four births already. My mother, Blanche, was 30 at the time;

my father, Byron, 38. A "Dr. Alfred R. Cobb" of Damascus, Ohio, signed my birth certificate. I am curious: was he actually in attendance? I was born at home and wonder, did my family merely summon Dr. Cobb by telephone? My eldest sibling, Florence, was 14. "Flo"— as she was known— already had her hands full helping Mother with Delmus, 8; Doris, 5; and Martha Elaine, only 2. What must the youngsters have thought of a new arrival? And Flo— as the eldest child-- was she looking forward to helping Mother with another newborn-- cooking, diapering, laundering, pampering— with... dread! Was it a time for celebration?

It was, after all, the famous holiday, Bastille Day.

I was born July 14, 1924, at 11:15 p.m., in my parents' house. Looking back—since my birth took place in the second story of our frame house in the middle of July— I imagine it was hot and sultry that night. Were Delmus, Doris and Martha Elaine (we call her "Elaine") all fast asleep or eagerly awake with the commotion?

Flo was likely in attendance to help Mother. Flo was a mere year shy of 15— Mother's same age when she had given birth to Flo.

As common with registries at the time, my birth certificate bore boxes for the Recorder to write in **RACE** and **"YES"** or **"NO"** under **LEGITIMATE**. It was recorded that drops were put into my eyes (Argyrol or other silver gelatin, administered to newborns, mandated after 1902 by state health departments as a gonorrheal prophylactic). Other statistics on my birth certificate state my father's occupation as "Carpenter" and my mother's as "Housewife."

July 14, 1924— there it was, right smack in the middle of the year. I have always been proud that my mother *born*ded me on that date. I associate the date 1) with my birth name, "Marcella" (Latin, by way of a layover in France); 2) with Bastille Day (July 14, 1789, the national holiday of the liberation of France); and 3) with "*La* Marcell-*aze*" (the national anthem of France, "La Marseillaise," spelled according to my young ears).

The next morning— how did Flo, Delmus, Doris and Elaine react? Did they awake sleepy-eyed, to find their new little sister in bed with Mother? Had anyone slept at all? Was a home birth a novelty or taken for granted?

Delmus at age 8 and Doris at age 5 were able to dress themselves. But Elaine, at 2, was dressed by big-sister Flo. What array of disarray disrupted my family's routine the next day, July 15th? How about my father? I know he didn't pass around cigars to his friends (unless he went up to the Lodge Hall later), but cigars cost money. He likely picked up his routine— his chores— milking the cow, feeding the chickens, slopping the hogs. Did he view me as just another mouth to feed?

I am certain, yes: another mouth to feed.

And Mother, God bless her. Home births in the 1920's were primitive. No anesthesia for my dear mother, no painkillers, no sophisticated antiseptic procedure for her and newborn. The slop bucket from the upstairs hallway (the family's overnight commode) was grabbed to serve as a receptacle for the afterbirth. With only home remedies at hand, how long was Mother sore and bleeding afterward?

Mother breastfed me. In 1924, there was no alternative (no infant formula) that we knew of. As a suckling infant during those times, I had no concept of the inconvenience my birth may have caused my family...

...which leads to speculation.

*Where did I sleep!* I have no recollection of a crib ever being in the big house, but there had to have been one. My parents could not have had me sleeping in their bed until I was old enough to bundle in with my sisters. The risk of being rolled over on would have been too great.

They put me in a box, quite likely-- a wooden box, with a quilt in it. I know we didn't have a *bassinette*, a cradle on rockers or any baby receptacle like they have now.

And my swaddling clothes-- did I have nightgowns and fitted undergarments? There <u>were</u> no undergarments, they were not even thought of. There were only diapers. And these? Diaper services and Pampers were not *born*ded yet. What did we use for diapers? I can only imagine. My mother might have bought yards of flannel material at the "5 & 10" in Salem— to cut into rectangles. Or she might've used sugar sacks, but those were not overly plentiful—and too coarse for a baby unless the fabric had been washed multiple times into softness.

Elaine was probably still in diapers when I was born. Did she toddle about the house in bare feet, diapers drooping, waiting to be changed?

A word about those sugar sacks. These were a godsend to rural mothers. In that era, sugar was available in 50-pound cloth bags. My frugal mother purchased sugar in bulk for canning a garden's worth of fruits and vegetables. In our home, there was always a 50-pound sack of sugar on the landing, half way up the stairs to the bedrooms. The white cotton cloth with dark blue printing was of a good, practical cut so it provided adequate cloth for home sewing projects. (In later years, ornery boys at Mill Creek School learned my humble underthings were made of sugar sacks when they yanked up my dress to peek— and to embarrass me.)

Thus began my life as the fifth child in our family. Did my family want me? I am going to tell myself they did. Flo took care of me, as she did my brother and sisters before me. She was six years older than Delmus and any chance of a leisurely childhood for her was cut short because of it. Another example of the bane of birth order.

Because Delmus was 8 when I was born he was old enough to fend for himself. Was he dismayed as the only boy among four girls? (He would have to wait two more years for a baby brother.)

Until I was 5, I have no recollection of my childhood. Flo, Delmus and Doris have passed away (in 2005, 1998 and 2007, respectively). My sister, Elaine, was only two years old when I was born. So, today, she cannot tell me about my early years. Was I cheerful, placid and well behaved; or colicky, irritable and whiney-- demanding and spoiled?

There is no one alive who can tell me.

# VIGNETTE: COCOA & HONEY.

BEING INQUISITIVE BUT OLD ENOUGH TO KNOW BETTER, I PULLED A CHAIR UP TO THE KITCHEN CUPBOARD WHERE MOTHER KEPT HER SPICES. I TOOK DOWN THE BOX OF HERSHEY'S COCOA POWDER. I PUT TWO HEAPING TABLESPOONS OF COCOA INTO A SAUCER. I WAS ANTICIPATING A REAL FEAST. I ADDED SEVERAL DOLLOPS OF HONEY TO IT AND STIRRED UP THE GOO.

"*M-MMM GOOD*," I THOUGHT.

*NOT GOOD.* I TOOK MY FIRST BITE. IT WAS BITTER BUT SWEET SO I ATE THE ENTIRE CONCOCTION. I WAS SOON TO KNOW IT WAS NOT THE TREAT I THOUGHT IT WAS GOING TO BE. I RAPIDLY BECAME SICK TO MY STOMACH. I WISHED SOMEONE HAD BEEN THERE TO HELP ME *NAUSEATE* INTO THE SINK. IF I'D A BEEN SMART I'D A MADE MYSELF THROW UP. BUT THE SHEER BITTERNESS AND SUGARYNESS OF IT—MADE ME THROW UP ANYWAY.

WHEN THIS CAPER BECAME KNOWN TO THE FAMILY (I HAD TO CONFESS WHEN THEY SAW ME THROWING UP) THEY DIDN'T LET IT REST FOR WEEKS.

"MARCELLA," THEY SAID, TEASINGLY—*OBLIGINGLY*--"WOULD YOU LIKE ANOTHER DISH OF COCOA AND HONEY?"

--C. 1932

# CHAPTER 3:
## MY IMMEDIATE FAMILY.

*"WE ONLY ARGUE WHEN WE HAVE A DIFFERENCE OF OPINION. "*
                                                    --JLG

*a*WKWARD" hardly begins to define the inception of my parents' married life together.

My father, "B.E. Woolf," was born April 7, 1886, in Fort Wayne, Indiana, to Howard Jerome and Martha Diehl Woolf. He was their first born.

My mother was Blanche Othel Cline. Her birth date was June 19, 1894. Her parents were Homer Cornelius and Jenny Sloan Cline. Blanche was a lifelong resident of Berlin Center, Ohio, where she was born.

Byron married Blanche February 23, 1910, under extreme duress. This is a fair assumption. Blanche was 15 at the time and Byron 23. Blanche's father, Homer Cline, had insisted that this ceremony take place (as told to me by Flo years later). When they married, Blanche was a week away from giving birth to Flo, their first child and my eldest sister— Florence Ethel Woolf. Flo was born March 2, 1910.

Blanche's first pregnancy surely was emotionally charged. Homer Cline succeeded in removing an impending stain of illegitimacy from the mix by forcing the couple to wed a week before Flo was born. The usual physical rigors of pregnancy were no doubt heightened by the emotional trauma of this stigma. I do not know how my parents met. I do know the Woolfs were a little better off financially than the Clines. The setting was 1910, in rural Ohio. This burden must have borne the sting of "community justice," intensified by my mother's mortified embarrassment and perhaps my father's resentment. Lord only knows how the couple began their wedded life under such inauspicious beginnings— with the cards stacked against them so.

Ours wasn't the first family that ever happened to.

Byron had been living in a moderate-sized farmhouse on Berlin Station Road, two roads up from (north of) Western Reserve Road. After the marriage vows, he and Blanche resided there together. In this farmhouse Florence was born.

Six years later my older brother, Delmus Florin Woolf, was born March 15, 1916. Surely Flo was made to assist in caring for her baby brother. Delmus, like his big sister, was delivered in this house on Berlin Station Road.

I have wondered why there was a six-year lapse between my parents' first and second child. Neither my mother nor father ever revealed to me a reason. Who knows what grudges or guilt (if at all) might have influenced such an abstinence?

My parents were doing the best they could.

The family of four Woolfs lived in the Berlin Station Road farmhouse until 1917. That was the year they purchased the house I grew up in— our "family home"-- on South Pricetown Road, a few hundred yards south of Western Reserve Road.

After the move to the larger farmhouse in 1917, life was challenging, especially for my mother. The big house, having been built in 1903, was still relatively new. The house overlooked 16 acres of farm land, the garage, outhouse, barn and the little graveyard tucked away in the upper northeast corner.

Of my parents' six children, we four youngest were born in this house. Doris Evelyn Woolf was born April 6, 1919. Martha Elaine Woolf followed three years later. Her birth date is June 23, 1922. The author was born Bastille Day, 1924. Our baby brother, Homer Howard Woolf, was born April 22, 1926.

Martha Elaine was named after my father's mother, Martha Diehl Woolf. Homer was named for our two grandfathers: my mother's dad (Homer Cline) and my father's dad (Howard Woolf). I do not know after whom or *whoms* Doris, Delmus and Florence were named.

The origin of my name is more glamorous. "Marcella Loraine," the handwritten entry on my birth certificate, is clearly French. Florence long claimed <u>she</u> named me. She was 14 years old in 1924, putting her as just having finished seventh grade at Goshen High School. Flo conceivably (pardon the pun) could have been studying French in seventh grade (she had repeated sixth grade) or had found the name in a magazine or novel. Early on, Flo cultivated an avid reading habit, so her claim is likely. My dad always maintained that he had named me.

In later life, I thought strongly I should have been a "Betsy Jean" but Marcella it was. My mother and father shortened it to "Marcell." No one nicknamed me further. "Florence" was shortened to "Flo;" "Delmus" remained "Delmus." "Doris" became "Dodie." "Martha Elaine" we shortened to "Elaine." And "Homer" was always "Homer." We all had a sense of homer—I mean, humor.

Growing up, I thought of myself and my place in our family as secure. Ours was a congenial family. Growing up I thought so and still think so.

I am sure my parents loved us all in our individual ways but "love" was freely acknowledged neither by parent nor child. Nobody ever said, "I love you" like they do today. However, love was there, not animosity. So perhaps it didn't need to be voiced.

We were not demonstrative. I didn't know any families who openly displayed their affections for each other.

Byron, my dad, was the boss in the family. He was not a strict disciplinarian. But his word was meant to be obeyed unequivocally. He'd say "No!" and that was the end of it. There was no follow-up. He meant what he said and said what he meant. Dad was rarely disputed. (Occasionally... begging on the part of us children allowed him to save face so he could relent.)

All of us respected his *rôle* as the one who made the decisions for the family.

My father was a hard worker and expected every one of us children— after we reached a certain age, say 6 or 7 or 8— to help out in the running of the farm.

Byron was a carpenter by trade and a talented one at that. He seemed suited to that line of work even though he silently fumed about the education stripped hard from him but handed easily to his younger brothers. Dad was flexible, *practical* and <u>ingenious</u>. He was amazing. Dad found solutions for every challenge by cleverly jury-rigging anything he could get his hands on. His innovations made life a lot easier for my mother and for the handling of our farm in general.

Somehow my mother or dad came up with an idea of far-reaching consequence. We ate better than most in that bleak time by virtue of this idea (or someone's suggestion) -- to start a poultry farm in 1930 or 1931 during the thick of the Depression.

Byron was friendly and had a gifted sense of humor that he handed down to all of us. He was not a reader of fiction but did enjoy his newspaper, The Youngstown Vindicator. Twenty-five miles northeast of Willow Run, Youngstown was the nearest metropolis. It was a thriving steel town, second only to Pittsburgh in production by 1921. In 1930, Youngstown's population peaked at 170,000. Dad had "the Vindy" (as we called it) delivered to the house. Carpentry jobs often took Dad to Youngstown for he routinely combed the classified ads in the Vindy for work. A carpenter named John Stewart (the father of our demoted helpmate, Martha) lived on Youngstown's west side. He and Dad often worked on the same projects together and they became friends. John and Dad became so thick that the Stewart family cultivated the ability to predict with near precision— give or take a fraction of a second-- the exact moment to pull into our driveway week after week as Mother was inches from setting hot, heaping platters of fried chicken on the table for Sunday dinner.

I wonder if my dad ever seriously considered working in the steel mills. I surmise he thought the carpentry trade was a step above working in the mills, which he thought of as geared toward immigrants. (Youngstown was dubbed the "Melting Pot" based on its population's high proportion of foreigners.)

Dad also read the Farm & Dairy journal; seed catalogues; the Sears, Roebuck catalogue (our bible) and assorted other trade publications.

Byron attended seventh grade off and on, until his father removed him permanently from further schooling to help on their family farm. For someone whose formal education was cut short so prematurely, Byron made a whopping success of our farm: at its zenith, Willow Run had more than 1,500 chickens— a mammoth enterprise.

Mother—Blanche-- was shy. She was out and out a sweet person. She was rarely outspoken or argumentative and had, instead, an enduring disposition. It was not that she was unflappable. She was. She got angry and felt put upon, but her moods did not last. At times, she could be swayed as far as begging and friendly persuasion went. But she never went so far as to overrule Dad's decisions; moreover, we kids knew enough not to ask her to.

Mother was hard working and dedicated to our family, as was my dad. They lived the Protestant work ethic. Mother's formal education ended in fifth grade. An eager reader (as much as time permitted), she enjoyed the newspaper, farm journals and periodicals Dad subscribed to. We had two bookcases in the living room but not too many books. Mother especially enjoyed The Saturday Evening Post, the Ladies' Home Journal and the Farm &

Dairy journal (if she could get it away from Dad). She clipped recipes from the journals, striving to put together savory home-cooked meals for us.

I always picture my mother wearing a bib apron she made from colorful material— red, orange, yellow, green and blue floral patterns. Her aprons had wide pockets in which she carried safety pins and always a crude homemade cotton hanky for wiping tears and runny noses.

Mother was the first one to rise in the morning. She arose at 6, dressed and went downstairs to the kitchen. The first order of business was to fire up the stove with coal and prepare a farmer's breakfast for all of us. My father followed within 10 minutes and shaved in the bathroom before we ate. Mother let us children sleep in. By 7 a.m., we were all seated at the kitchen table— effortlessly lured there by the smells of Mother's tantalizing home-cooked breakfasts.

Of all the people I have met around the world, my mother was the most generous and gentle person I have ever known.

---

ALL I AM, OR HOPE BE, I OWE TO
MY ANGEL MOTHER.

--ABRAHAM LINCOLN

Homer quickly became my best pal. As youngsters, we were inseparable. Elaine had a cackle of a laugh (and still does) -- a wonderful sense of humor. Dodie was a gentle, good-natured and unassuming person as amicable as they come. Delmus was quiet and studious. He was clever like my dad around tools and broken-down equipment. Flo was indispensable. She helped raise us children and assisted Mother. A great comfort to Mother, Flo was much more than just a second pair of hands.

Whatever burdens weighed down Blanche and Byron in their early married life, whatever recriminations may have erupted from being forced to marry each other— they seemed to reconcile privately, through time— each in their own way, quietly.

My parents' marriage of 56 years ended with Blanche's death in 1966.

No one in my family was lazy. My father <u>never</u> accepted public Relief like some of our neighbors—despite the fact that the Government tried to push it on everybody. We all were hard workers, education-minded, God-fearing and respectable folk.

# VIGNETTE: TEASING THE BULL.

*a* FAMILY HIRED DORIS FOR HOUSEWORK WHEN SHE WAS 16. HOMER AND I WERE TOO YOUNG TO BE HIRED OUT SO WE CONTINUED OUR PLAYING, INDUSTRIOUSLY MARAUDING UPON THE NEIGHBORS AND HAVING FUN. THE STRATTON'S FARM WAS SOUTH ON ROUTE 534, THE FIRST FARM ON THE WEST SIDE OF THE ROAD. WE ALWAYS SNUCK IN THE BACK WAY TO LOU STRATTON'S BARN TO TEASE HIS JERSEY BULL. WE SAT ON THE BARS OF THE STALL AND POKED THE POOR BEAST WITH A STICK. THIS WAS QUITE A LONG STICK FOR OBVIOUS REASONS, PROBABLY ABOUT FIVE FOOT LONG. OUR PRODDING MADE THE BULL SNORT AND PAW THE STRAW BEDDING INTO FURROWS THAT EXPOSED THE DIRT FLOOR. IT WAS MEAN OF US TO DO THIS AND NOT AT ALL NICE. THE BULL HAD A BIG METAL RING IN HIS NOSE. WE WERE FASCINATED ALSO BY HIS PENDULATIONS.

MOTHER NEVER FOUND OUT WE DID THIS. WE NEVER BRAGGED TO A SOUL THAT WE WERE BEING CRUEL TO AN ANIMAL. NO DOUBT MOTHER WOULD AGREE IT WAS UNKIND OF US AND BRAZENLY DANGEROUS. WE COULD HAVE TUMBLED INTO THE STALL AND BEEN TRAMPLED OR GORED. HAD SHE KNOWN, MOTHER WOULD HAVE SAID, CHARACTERISTICALLY: "DON'T EVER DO IT AGAIN."

HOMER AND I ALSO HELD CONTESTS. IN ONE, WE SWIPED A BEE OR WASP IN OUR PALMS TO SEE HOW LONG BEFORE ONE OF US GOT STUNG.                                                    --C. 1935

***

I WAS REMINDED RECENTLY HOW DANGEROUS JERSEY BULLS ARE. THE MALE JERSEY IS NO COUNTERPART TO THE DOCILE FEMALE SUCH AS BORDEN'S GENTLE, DOE-EYED ELSIE THE COW IN POPULAR ADVERTISING. A MENNONITE GENTLEMAN AT OUR FARMERS MARKET TOLD MY CO-AUTHOR THAT MOST OF HIS CONTEMPORATIES (MEN IN THEIR LATE 40'S) HAD BEEN KILLED— EACH GORED BY THEIR JERSEY BULL. HE DESCRIBED THE DAIRY BULL—AMONG ALL BREEDS—ASTONISHINGLY, AS THE MOST AGGRESSIVE AND PROTECTIVE OF THE COWS IN ITS CHARGE.

# The House: The Physical Layout.

# CHAPTER 4:
## THE BASEMENT.

*"GET INTO THE ROUNDHOUSE NELLY,*
*HE CAN'T CORNER YOU THERE!"*

--DAD

M Y dad used to say that about innocent little Nelly, without provocation.

We kids never knew what he meant but we giggled anyway when he said it. It just felt funny. We were too young to figure it out. No doubt Dad thought it quite funny, as he said it often enough. My mother had an actual friend in Berlin Center named Nelly Renkenberger. She was a buxom lass. She wasn't a "lass"— she was a woman, with chubby cheeks and a double chin and flabby upper arms and thick ankles. Whenever Dad spouted his little Nellyism, I imagined Mother's Nelly R. cowering up against a wall with some no-do-gooder creeping toward her – up to no good. I had no good idea what "no good" entailed, but I assumed it was no good. And our villain does need worry--Mother's pal Nelly was stout enough to take care of herself.

Nelly R. would have knocked his block off.

Our house, always painted white, had a full basement— which we alternately called a "cellar." This is where my description of the house begins.

The cellar wasn't round, Nelly!

Come up the back steps through the screen door. Make a good effort not to slam it. Slog through the kitchen gingerly with your muddy boots and try not to leave behind a straw-covered clod of chicken manure on Mother's clean floor. Head cater-corner, to the cellar door. This leads directly down to three steps, then a landing. Directly in front of you is an outside door with a square pane of glass. We rarely used this door as it led to the side yard where there were not much goings-on. This outer door had a deadbolt that we kept locked.

The landing was larger than expected because a casement built onto the north side of the house enlarged its depth. (The casement rose to enclose the upstairs landing equally.) Outside, an endearing, peaked roof with slate tiles covered the casement. This structure came original to the house and effectively doubled the space of the landings for the cellar and second floor. The casement did not extend up beyond the main roof.

In the cellar landing, my dad had hung plain-board shelves on its small east wall. Here we kept hats, mittens, scarves and other outdoor paraphernalia. Under the shelves we stored boots and shoes. On the opposite wall were hooks from sea to shining sea (doorway to doorway) for aprons, coats, jackets, overalls and work jackets. And it was a favorite spot for Dad to hammer some nails into when he got bored.

Turning to the right, a series of 11 additional steps led into the basement proper. The steps ended in the northeast corner of the basement. In the northwest corner was a section my father built to enclose the furnace and its coal stores. We called this "the furnace room." Its floor— as was the entire basement floor— was hard-packed dirt. A wooden door led into the furnace room. There was ample space for the coal-burning furnace. Provision was laid out on the north side of this room for coal that lay in a pile about five feet high when freshly delivered. We phoned the coal man to come by when our supply dwindled to a dangerous level-- we did not dare let it run out. Our Ohio winters were hard.

We did not need to use the furnace in summer.

It fell to everyone to stoke the furnace, including my mother. She was not above that. She was home alone all day and could not dare let the furnace go out.

The furnace sat in the free space in the center of this small room. Aside from the kitchen stove, the furnace was the sole source of heat for the entire house. In the main part of the house, four floor registers could be adjusted with a slide to control the amount of warm air flowing up from the furnace beneath: downstairs, in the living room, the kitchen and in my father's office (in the corner near his roll-top desk); and, on the second floor-- the only register up there was in the bedroom directly above the living area (this bedroom of course went to my parents).

The black furnace was tall— about 6 foot high by 5 foot wide. It was manufactured of cast iron. In its center was a rectangular door about a foot high by 15 inches wide, which opened directly into the insatiable cavity of the furnace. Even though the handle was made of a metal coil (to wick away heat), the door handle could become hot enough to sear a careless hand— we had to use a rag on the handle to avoid a severe burn. The furnace room was no place for inattentiveness or horseplay. We employed a shovel to scoop coal off the floor and slung the load into the furnace— the door was in the back facing the northwest corner. Whoever installed the furnace was to be congratulated because the door opened to the right, with the coal bin situated to the left. This made feeding the fiery but benevolent dragon easier.

We kids were entrusted to this dreaded task after age 6 or 7.

And it was dreaded.

"One of you kids go down an' throw a couple shovelfuls of coal into the furnace," Dad said, nightly.

"It's yer turn," we replied in unison, looking at each other dumbly.

"I did it last time," Elaine said.

"No ya didn't, I did!" Dodie said.

"No sir!" I said. "I did."

"I'll go down if you go down with me," Elaine said.

"Quit arguing and just do it," Dad said. "Marcell, go with her."

That was that.

We had to beg each other to do it. None of us youngsters eagerly jumped up to leave the comfort of the warm living room to go into the basement with its dark corners harboring who knew what? Who knew? Nelly's wax-mustachioed *perpitraticor* could have been lurking in the shadows. It was black as coal over there by the furnace room. And if it were nighttime (<u>especially</u> at night) it was spooky. I was wary of villains and fretted constantly if the cellar windows were locked.

A particularly odious task usually fell to my older brother. The furnace interior held a slotted grate that bore chunks of coal but allowed ashes to fall through. My brother, Delmus, had to clean these ashes out of the bottom of the furnace. He stored the ashes in a trio of five-gallon tar buckets. These metal buckets stood right in front of the furnace. They were quite handy. On occasion, someone used one of the ash buckets to pee in (actually, it was more than occasionally). This infuriated Delmus but it saved the offending party a trip to the outhouse on a winter night. When the buckets got full (of... ashes) he carried them upstairs, through the kitchen and out the back door. Delmus distributed the ashes onto our unpaved driveway—it helped keep down the mud.

Near the east wall of the cellar was a well. It had been dug and framed-in when the house was built. In fact— assuredly the house was built around this well. The well provided our bathing, cleaning, cooking, drinking and clothes-washing water.

The well down cellar often went dry in summer. During a rainy year, the well was fine.

The well had a square, concrete collar that was wide enough to sit on. An electric Delco pump sat on this collar. Water was pumped to the kitchen and bathroom sinks, and to the bathtub, all on the first floor. Only the cellar and first floor had running water. A noisy gasoline generator fueled this pump before Berlin Center ran electricity past our house. There was also a hand pump there at the well. Water was originally delivered by pipes solely to the kitchen sink. My dad extended this system when he converted the kitchen pantry to a bathroom soon after moving into the house in 1917. (He was astonishingly handy with these little tricks.)

These were the only two rooms with access to water in the upstairs, then-- the kitchen and the bathroom.

In the middle of the cellar originated a free-standing brick chimney that extended straight up through the kitchen into the second floor. This chimney was not related to heating purposes, as our house had no fireplace. Rather, the chimney served to vent, via flumes, waste gasses (from furnace and stove) up through the roof.

Hugging the chimney on its south side was an encasement for a clothes chute. This luxury obviated the *trudgery* of carrying dirty laundry down cellar, a convenience that spared hundreds of trips down one or two flights of stairs. We had easy access to the laundry chute in the kitchen and in the second-story hallway. Compliments again due the designer of our house.

From the walls around the well and extending southward hung clotheslines my mother used fall and winter. During clement weather she hung clothes outside. At the bottom of the steps was a washtub and scrub board which sat on a small table my dad had built close to the well. He also provided Mother a comfort on the east wall near the foot of the steps: a faucet that piped water over from the well. The tub had a hand-cranked wringer mounted to the side of the tub, to squeeze water out of the clothes after they were washed. Eventually, Dad bought Mother a proper electric wringer-washer appliance.

Washday fell on Monday. For my mother— with a family of eight— this was a Sisyphean task: repetitive and unrelenting. Sheets from four beds, pillowcases, overalls, shirts, underwear, dirty socks, table cloths, dresses, aprons, towels-- tremendous and unrewarding hard labor for her, never ending.

Beyond the clotheslines was an area beneath a small window on the south wall, where Mother handled eggs. Even before my folks opened our poultry farm, we raised chickens. In this area of the cellar, Mother cleaned and sorted the eggs. In later years, when we stopped buying baby chicks and started hatching our own, candling was added to Mother's egg-handling job.

A drain in the cellar floor, coupled with the hand pump and relative warmth of the space in winter, made the basement a suitable, sanitary workplace for processing eggs. No wonder Mother spent so much time down there.

No one handled eggs but her.

Also in this particular area were sturdy four-inch hooks screwed into the floor joists overhead. From the pigs we butchered, we hung hams and bacon and shoulders, to air-cure for a few months.

Later, say 1942, on the east wall behind the well, my father built a door to the outside. To save space in the cellar, he cleverly built this door into the basement wall and excavated outward in order to install the steps outdoors. (Had he built this exit back in the 1920's or 30's, it would have spared countless muddy boot tracks left on the kitchen floor.) This innovation afforded Mother easier egress for carrying wash outdoors to dry and ease of ingress for returning to the house with a large basket of newly gathered eggs from the laying house.

Why didn't Dad install that **&#$%** door sooner!?

In the southwest corner of the basement was the prize plum, the fruit cellar. It was extensive. Dad had provisioned the walls with wide and deep shelves. To Mother's credit, these shelves were filled with row upon row of glass Ball jars, sometimes four or five jars deep— filled with delectables. By the quart and pint jar, she canned the vegetables and fruit we grew. Dad also bought fruit for Mom to can. There were quart jars of beef she cooked and canned in its own broth...

...talk about a special treat in winter.

The variety of fruit and vegetables from our farm provided a cornucopia of hearty eating for our table the year 'round. Mother canned a lot of tomatoes from our kitchen garden. Quarts of beets, green beans and lima beans lined the shelves alongside pint jars of carrots. She put up a variety of pickles made from cucumbers we grew.

The fruit my mother put up was especially savory. I can just picture them now— the peaches, for instance. Oh! The peaches. Ambrosia.

She also canned plump, juicy, sweet blackberries in quart jars. Other homegrown delicacies were walnut-sized purple plums she canned. These too were an indulgence.

She made apple sauce and apple butter from bushels of Jonathan or MacIntosh apples my dad bought or bartered from our neighbors.

To this day I do not eat apple butter.

Mother canned cherries. Were they good. They were red sour cherries. What I would give for a slice of Mother's home-baked cherry pie.

Then there were the jams, jellies and preserves. These tasted so good on Mother's homemade bread with her sweet butter.

We canned all this food because we could not afford a refrigerator or freezer back then to keep food from spoiling. The only cooler at that time was our icebox in the kitchen upstairs. The icebox only had a bit of room for milk. What we couldn't eat we had to preserve or let go to waste.

---

**W**E ATE FOOD TO PRESERVE IT. WE ATE WHAT WE COULD AND WHAT WE COULDN'T EAT WE CANNED.

In the center of the fruit cellar, we stored root vegetables, cabbages, pumpkins and winter squash. The basement was cool enough in summer but warm enough in winter to conserve (but not freeze) the produce.

In a separate place, over near a support post holding up the ceiling, we stored Mother's sauerkraut.

This then was the basement of our family home. The warmest part of the house because it was underground— the basement provided a cozy haven for Mother's egg factory; storage or curing space for vegetables, fruits and meat we produced; and a laundry-processing area for my family's *Herculeaps* of dirty clothes and bedding.

# VIGNETTE: CLOSE NEIGHBORS.

*i* WAS A TOMBOY. I CLIMBED TREES AND ENJOYED DOING THINGS THE BOYS DID. I ALWAYS WANTED TO BE A BOY. HOMER AND I DRESSED ALIKE (ME IN BOYS' CLOTHES, NOT HIM IN GIRLS' CLOTHES) IN BIB OVERALLS. ACROSS THE ROAD FROM THE CEMETERY WAS A SHABBY HOUSE. A FAMILY NAMED ROEPKE LIVED THERE. MY FOLKS THOUGHT OF THEM AS SLOVENLY AND VULGAR. THEY HAD TWO BOYS, OUR AGES. THE OLDER BOY'S NAME WAS ARTHUR. MOTHER AND DAD STRICTLY FORBADE US TO HAVE ANY CONSORT WITH THIS FAMILY, ESPECIALLY THESE TWO BOYS. IF HOMER AND I WENT UP TO THE PLUM ORCHARD TO PICK FRUIT OR ONLY TO FOOL AROUND, THE BOYS CAME RUNNING ACROSS THE ROAD. ARTHUR KEPT HARANGUING ME: "ARE YOU A BOY OR A GIRL?" HE ASKED. "I'M A BOY," I SAID. "CAN'T YOU TELL!" "NO," HE SAID, "I THINK YOU'RE A GIRL." TO PROVE THIS ONE DAY, I PUT MY HAND INTO THE BIB OF MY OVERALLS AND STUCK MY INDEX FINGER THROUGH THE FLY AND WIGGLED MY FINGER. I SAID, "SEE, THAT PROVES IT, I'M A BOY." THE ROEPKE BOYS LOOKED DUM(B)FOUNDED BUT SEEMED TO ACCEPT THE FACT THAT I WAS A BOY. (GOSH, MY FACE IS RED JUST TELLING THIS.) ARTHUR NEVER HAD A CHANCE TO HECKLE ME AGAIN. WE NEVER DARED GO NEAR THEM AGAIN-- THAT WAS OUR LAST ENCOUNTER WITH THIS FAMILY. FOR, WHEN WE RETURNED FROM THE PLUM ORCHARD, I HAD TO BRAG ABOUT MY RUSE. DAD WAS FURIOUS. "I TOLD YOU DON'T EVER HAVE ANY TRUCK WITH THAT TRASH." (WE HAD KEPT SNEAKING BACK UP THERE— THEY FASCINATED US.) THE CONSEQUENCES THIS TIME WERE SWIFT AND EFFECTIVE. THIS WAS THE LAST STRAW. IT WAS SUMMER AND WE WERE OUTSIDE WHEN THE TRUTH BECAME KNOWN. DAD STRIPPED OFF SWITCHES FROM THE PRIVET HEDGE AND REALLY LICKED US GOOD ON OUR LEGS, OUR BUTTS AND OUR BACKS. "THAT WILL TEACH-YA," HE SAID, "TO NOT EVER DO THAT AGAIN." AND WE NEVER DID. ANOTHER OCCASION FOR US TO GO RUNNING TO MOTHER, SOBBING, CRYING OURSELVES TO SLEEP ON THE DAVENPORT. SUCH WAS LIFE.                    –C.1930

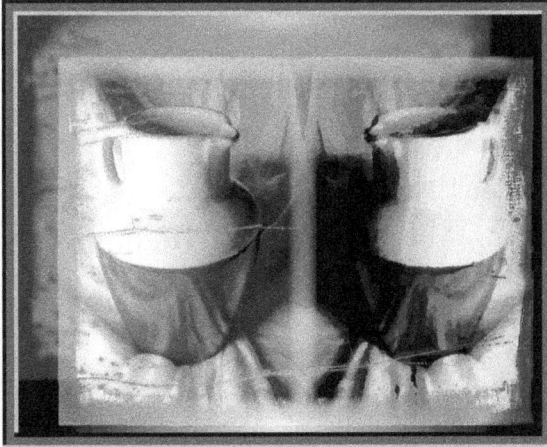

# CHAPTER 5:
## THE DOWNSTAIRS.

*--"BLANCHE, I NEED TO GREASE THE TRACTOR.*
*DO YOU HAVE ANY RAGS?"*
*--"YES, BYRON, I'M <u>WEARING</u> THEM."*

**t**HE stairs at the north end of the basement led up to the spacious landing. To the left, the three steps led into the kitchen. To the right the solid wooden door led outdoors. White with lime-green trim, the door was seldom used as an access or exit, as it led nowhere. The driveway and outbuildings were on the other side of the house, the south side.

The kitchen occupied a 14-by-20 foot space in the northeast corner of the house. It was a typically-big farmhouse kitchen. Half a dozen entryways led into the kitchen, the heartland of our home.

A screen door led in to the kitchen from the porch, at the center of our home's east wall. Immediately to the left was the bathroom door on the south wall. Right next to it was the door leading in from what we always called "Dad's room." On the west wall was a doorless entryway leading from the living room. The cellar door faced north adjacent to the living room portal. The sixth door led upstairs (the cellar and upstairs steps shared the same casement, thus the door leading to the bedrooms above faced west at the north part of the kitchen).

The kitchen had only two windows. This pair of large, square windows shared the northeast corner.

With the aroma of bread baking in the oven... that sweet smell of Mom's homemade bread... a tour of the downstairs begins with the most frequented room in the house: the bathroom.

And, it was truly a <u>bath</u> room: only a sink and tub-- no built-in toilet there or anywhere in the house.

The bathroom was about 6 by 9 foot and that's probably stretching it a bit. The door opened outward into the kitchen to allow more room inside the elbow-bumping space. Its floor was laid with one-inch, octagonal white ceramic tile. The walls were plastered and painted white. They were always painted white. A small window on the east wall opposite the sink opened only six inches. Two small metal chains kept it from falling down against the wall, for the window was hinged at the bottom so as to flop open from the top.

This window was covered with a heavy poster board— heavy cardboard— which featured a lady flourishing a Camel cigarette in her right hand, arm extending in a salute of feminine liberty. (One might assume she was a "lady.") The poster was replete with advertising. She sported a beige, trend-setting cloche hat that hugged her blonde, bobbed hair. Her round-collared dress was also beige.

The poster was done in yellows, browns and tans.

In a family of eight, someone is always watching you and what you're doing (or not doing). In turn, this demure maven spied on all of us in a place (the bathroom) that otherwise should have been the only haven in the entire house where a person could savor a few moments of privacy. This earth-toned flapper was unflappable about her spying.

The tub was set against the back wall. It was not a claw-foot tub. It sat on the floor like bathtubs do today.

The sink, with no cabinet underneath, was attached to the west wall opposite the window. There, hung a rectangular mirror in a maple frame. I'd like to think there was a cabinet behind the mirror for Dad's shaving paraphernalia. Our Camel lady had the doubly-delicious delight of gazing at our occasional bathroom exigencies but also at herself in the mirror all day long.

Dad's razor strop hung from a hook on the door jamb. The leather strop was used to sharpen his straight razor and to punish us children.

There was always a towel made of the ubiquitous sugar-sack material, hanging on a nail on the window frame. We had to turn around to wipe our hands after using the sink, while throwing a wink at the Camel girl. It was a little unhandy to drip over the floor on the way to the towel. With the eight of us, the towel got dirty quick.

Why my otherwise-industrious dad waited to install a toilet (and that outside door for the basement) in the bathroom until every single one of us six kids had left home-- remains a perplexity, the true riddle of the Sphinx. Perhaps a lack of money or adequate water from our well (or both) prevented him from doing so earlier.

The fact remains: during my entire childhood and adolescence, we never had a permanent toilet indoors (the slop bucket upstairs did not count).

Next to the bathroom was a wooden door leading from Dad's room. This door opened oddly into his office while the bathroom door opened into the kitchen. The door to Dad's office swung open against the east wall. The floor in his office was tongue-and-groove oak laid out in a north-south direction. The plaster walls were painted white (what else?). A pair of average-sized windows complimented the south wall. A second door on the far west wall led into the living room. The white ceiling was plastered as in a modern home. A single lightbulb hung from the ceiling with a pull string to turn it on and off. There was no globe on the lightbulb fixture.

The only closet downstairs was in my dad's office. The closet measured 6 by 9 foot, it hosted sturdy cast-iron hooks on all four sides, including the side the door was on, and plenty of nails hammered into the walls. My dad's heavy sheepskin coat typically hung there on the south wall. Here we kept our winter coats. We stored articles other than clothing in there too. For instance, my uncle Emerson's gas mask from the "Great War" (World War I) hung on a hook or lay on the floor. We kids always put the mask on just for fun. Some boxes sat on the floor. Who knows what was in them? A shelf on the north wall doubled as a corn-drying area in late summer. The closet contained no light fixture.

My father's office held his oak rolltop desk, in the northwest corner. A bank of drawers lined up on each side of the desk's kneehole like side-lights framing an old doorway. The desk also had a single drawer in the center. In the rows of small drawers and pigeonholes up top, Dad filed away correspondence, bills he had paid, pencils, paper clips, three-cent stamps and penny postcards— no letter opener, no stapler. (Staplers had been invented in the 1800's but we never had one. If we wanted to attach two pieces of paper together, we used a straight pin.) On the desk top, Dad kept a stack of farm journals and a sweet little postal scale.

To the right of my father's desk, a calendar always hung on the wall on a nail. Dad-the-carpenter was always hammering a nail into something. (To this day I do the same thing.) The oversized calendar with large, easy-to-read numbers, usually came from Hawkins Mill— from whence came our chicken feed. Dad relied on the calendar. We all did.

At his desk, Dad used a bent-back chair. It was made of oak and painted gray, with a hard seat and no cushion. Rungs supported the back. The floor was bare, no carpet, no throw rugs. Scrape-marks accumulated on the floor over the years, indicating where Dad habitually had pushed back his chair.

Extra chairs lined the walls in this room.

My mother's sewing machine stood against the east wall. It was not an electric model. To operate it, Mother worked a foot pedal. The ceiling light was the only light fixture available for Mother's sewing. Two wicker clothesbaskets filled with different types of material sat behind the door, adjacent to the sewing machine. Mother made quilts and she kept fabrics and remnants of material in these baskets.

The office also held an oak library table that sat on the south wall. It was impressive, constructed with a drawer in the center and a shelf at the bottom between the legs. The shelf was about a foot wide and extended the length of the table underneath. We kept nothing on this shelf. It was purely decorative. The tabletop was a repository for junk— items that did not have a place anywhere else: crumpled-up clothes, sweaters. No kid's toys! (Who had any toys! Not us.) An old Sears, Roebuck catalogue could have been lying there.

A new Sears, Roebuck & Company catalogue came each spring and fall. We eagerly awaited it. We did our shopping through this catalogue. The new one supplanted the previous catalogue, which—outdated— was destined for infamy by being proudly carted off to the outhouse behind the garage.

Dad had built a small, low stand for Mother's houseplants. He made it from pine, sturdy but undecorated, for Mother's coleus, asparagus ferns and other houseplants. I have no idea if they bought these plants at Hawkins or if a friend of Mother's supplied her with cuttings.

Mother loved her plants and was proud of them. She was a good gardener as far as houseplants and her garden were concerned.

Alongside the plant table in the southwest corner of Dad's office was a hall tree he had made, although we did not have a hall. The single post was four-by-four oak and stood about six foot tall. He decorated it with four flared feet that lent a sophisticated look. At the top, he installed four big hooks where we hung our "good" coats.

In this room, temporary clotheslines stretched from wall to wall to dry clothes in winter and during inclement weather in the summer. We still had to have clean, dry clothes. On the way to the closet to get a coat or on the way to the table to pick up a book-- we had to wend our way through clothes and sheets drying there on the lines.

On the south wall above the library table hung a musket-loader rifle. That was kind of a barrier there— the table— to keep us kids from touching the gun, playing with it, trying to get it off the wall. We could have, but we were forbidden to. I do not know how my dad acquired this gun but I do know the disposition of it. That gun was his prized possession. He never fired it.

Dad's beloved rifle came to an unhappy ending. During an outbreak of scarlet fever circa 1931, Dad had to forfeit his pride and joy— this rifle— to pay the doctor. The whole affair was sad and left my dad heartbroken.

Leading off Dad's room, a doorway next to the hall tree led to our large living room that took up the entire west half of the house.

The living room, then, completes the layout of the first floor. We frequented this room evenings after supper.

The original floor plan allowed for one large room in the front of the house. The builder of the house—who lived there until my family moved in-- situated two bookcases in the center of this large room to carve out an additional room. The bookcases did not reach the ceiling. They jutted out toward each other, leaving an opening not sealed by a door. This portal led into what we called the "living room" in the northwest quadrant of the house.

The southwest quadrant we simply designated "the parlor." Originally it was set aside as a room to hold a casket for calling hours, but we never used it for that. (Willa Cather's novels are full of references to wakes held in family parlors for deceased sons, wives, fathers, daughters, infants—no funeral homes back then.)

The parlor contained a couch against the east wall, a wooden rocker and several "good" chairs. We kids were forbidden to sit in these plush chairs. Right in the center of the south wall was a moderate-sized window of the same dimensions as the pair in Dad's room. In front of this window was another plant stand Mother positioned there to take advantage of the light. Another window on the west wall (a large one) overlooked the front porch.

The parlor was separated from the living room only by those two attractive bookcases. Made of oak, each was about five foot tall and two foot across. Fronting each bookcase was a leaded-glass door, whose diagonal pattern lent a look of class. This pair of bookcases held about 10 books all told and Mother's knickknacks.

The passageway created by the bookshelves opened into the living room, occupying the northwest quarter of the house. Our front door, a solid-wood door with the knob on the left, led onto the front porch. Another large, matching window faced the porch to the north side of the front door.

In the living room, our family gathered after supper to read, play cards or listen to the radio, while Mother did some stitching by hand.

Whereas the basement was our home's center of industry, and the kitchen the hub, the living room was the focal point of our leisure. I can just picture Mother pulling the string on the kitchen light, after she was through with the supper dishes-- about to retire to the living room. Whoever had stayed behind to help Mother do dishes was anxious to join the others in the living room too. We couldn't wait to get in there after the kitchen was cleaned up. The living room was the most lived-in part of our house.

Figure 2: **RCA VICTOR RADIO.**
ILLUSTRATION BY M. GRENGA.

The fixture in the living room was our radio. It was not a luxury for us to have a radio. It was a necessity. Radios were cleverly priced (relatively) cheaply, perhaps a little over thirty dollars apiece (and, along with most Americans, we were a captive audience for the advertisements).

An RCA Victor, our radio was about 18 inches high with a Gothic-style peaked top colloquially called a "cathedral" radio. It was brown with vertical slots on the top half where the sound came out. It had an off-on—volume knob and a tuning knob— that was it, just those two. It plugged into the wall with an ugly brown cloth cord. The radio sat on a small wooden table (that my dad either made or bought) just inside the entrance to the kitchen. In the evening we listened to our favorite shows and eagerly followed serials aired week after week, from Jack Armstrong to the acerbic Father Coughlin.

The living-room furniture included an oak library table similar to the one in Dad's room. It sat underneath the large window in the north wall. My little brother hid under that table during lightning storms. There were also two old, black wicker rocking chairs. One was designated solely as "Dad's chair" and the only time we were allowed to sit in it was when he was absent. Whenever he came in and caught us in his chair, he swatted us with his newspaper.

"Get outta my chair!" he said. It did not take much to convince us.

The other rocker was rather Mom's chair in that she shared it with us. She was generous that way. Padded seats and backs enhanced the comfortableness of this pair of wicker rockers. The fabric of the pads was a floral print on chintz. We wore them out so Mother had to reupholster the cushions periodically. That took a lot of doing, the re-sewing. But it always brightened up the room when the new chair covers were displayed.

When our shows were on, we kids sat on straight-backed wooden chairs with cane seats. These chairs and the twin wicker rockers were clustered around the radio.

At some point, say 1932, Dad removed the bookcases-as-partitions, in order to restore this half of the house to one big, open living room. He relocated the bookcases so that they skirted either side of that large window in the now-dismantled parlor.

The entrance to the kitchen from the living room had no door. The doorway was framed-out but evermore lacked a door. It was unique. At the top was a three-inch dowel that held two forest-green drapes, heavier than cotton. They were drapery material (whatever that is). Soft material but heavier than just cotton, not canvas— it was a soft material but a heavy, soft material— in other words, it had substance. (It's so hard to describe. I'm still trying to think what kind of material that was.) In the winter these drapes were pulled together to keep the warmth within the living room. In summer the drapes were tied back with tasseled cords.

**W**HEN WE WERE TALL ENOUGH, WE CHINNED OURSELVES ON
THE DOWEL, MUCH TO MOTHER'S CONSTERNATION,
THAT'S A FACT. CAN YOU PICTURE US SWINGING THERE LIKE
TRAPEZE ARTISTS?

Flush with the living room floor, a metal register (about 9 by 12 inches in dimension) lay to the right of the kitchen entry and above the furnace. In winter, we kids huddled around this register.

On the east side of the living room, in the wall it shared with the kitchen, stood the lone chimney. It was narrow, not more than two foot wide. Commonly, homes in our region lacked fireplaces because of the dearth of firewood. (Ohio is deforested. Ohio's farmland and coal mines had been hewn out of virgin forest more than 100 years ago. Anecdotally-- before the 19th century, a squirrel could have run from the Ohio River to Lake Erie on the canopy of treetops without touching ground. No more.) The chimney vented only the cellar furnace and the kitchen stove.

The kitchen was cozy. It certainly survived many delicious meals. Our circular kitchen table was made from the omnipresent oak. This varnished, drop-side table came complete with two extra leaves to accommodate visitors (welcome and unwelcome alike; both graced us with their presence). When fully extended it truly was large— the table, not the visitors. (Come to think of it, some of them were large, too.)

Until 1929, our entire family sat at this table for meals (that same year, Flo left home to attend college). Mother kept it covered with a colorful oilcloth or with a cloth made from the all-present sugar sacks.

This table sat in the northeast corner of the kitchen, next to the buffet—more toward the window on the east wall.

One of us kids set the table each evening about 5:30, with sets of eight (if Flo was home) plates, knives, forks, spoons and glasses for water or milk. Salt and pepper shakers and a sugar bowl always sat in the center of the table-- we never removed these except to change the tablecloth. Four high-backed chairs with hard, paperboard seats were reserved for my parents, Flo and Delmus. We four younger children sat on hard, bent-back chairs.

We never had napkins.

At 6:00 p.m., everyone but Mother sat down. She brought the dishes over to the table that she had prepared earlier at the stove. She did this so the meal was served hot. We always had one type of meat, several vegetables, fresh-baked bread with churned butter, chilled fresh milk (as long as the ice held out) and a homespun dessert or two.

We ate like the House of Windsor, *sans* servants.

Like the clothes chute, another much-appreciated domestic innovation was a cabinet for a fold-up ironing board built into the kitchen wall. You really have to give that Sumner Stanley credit for designing that neat trick (or Sears, if he used their popular mail-order house plans). The ironing-board cupboard was so cute. It was housed in the east wall between the window and the screen door. It served its purpose well. Its tall pine door opened to the left. A spring-latch lock secured the door. The ironing board was hinged at the bottom and swung down for use, supported underneath by wood struts. It stowed upright in the wall to save kitchen space.

Mother did most of the ironing with an electric Sunbeam. She spent hours and hours ironing loads of clothes there by the kitchen table.

Rounding the Horn from the triad of doors (to the back porch, bathroom and Dad's room) -- a tall, white wooden stool sat left of the stove. I spent many an hour as a child sitting on that stool watching Mother cook.

The stove was a behemoth. It commanded the kitchen. Providing heat for cooking and the boiling of water, it also warmed the kitchen fall, winter and spring. However, the same effect was not as appreciated in summer: a broiling hot kitchen!

The stove was catercorner from the kitchen table. It was a wood-burning stove that we burned coal in, as pointed out. We did not have enough wood on our farm to burn for fuel, nor the money had firewood been available. We brought a bucket of coal up from the pile down cellar. The bucket always sat on the floor to the right of the stove. A workhorse-- that was our stove. It was a housewife's pride, like Dad's musket-loader. Built of cast iron, the stove had four burners, two water reservoirs, an oven bay and a warming hood. Of course, there was the ash pit that we had to empty daily. The stove was a real work of art— black with grey trim. A reservoir for boiling water was on either side. We poured water from the sink into the reservoirs and the stove heated the water. It was really nice to have piping-hot water to carry back to the sink to clean greasy dishes and pots and skillets.

The oven was spacious and certainly proved its mettle by producing thousands of home-baked custards, pies and loaves of bread in its lifetime.

Mother was not a cake baker.

The oven door was hinged at the bottom (like the bathroom window) so we pulled it forward to open. The open door provided a place to set already-hot dishes or pans to keep warm while Mother prepared the rest of the meal. The oven had two racks but no broiler.

Up top, the built-in hood had a pair of sliding glass doors, behind which was room to keep additional dishes warm until serving time. When feeding eight people, a lot of space is needed to keep food warm. Fried chicken, mashed potatoes, hot pies, puddings —any dish appropriate to keep warm until serving time benefited from these features.

There was no griddle on the stove top.

How did Mother light the stove? What we called "burners" were actually flat, round, cast-iron lids. Each had a squared-off notch on top to accommodate a specially designed tool that came with the stove. This check-mark-shaped tool was a lifting handle, also cast iron. Like the furnace door, its handle was coiled to keep it cool. It only got hot if carelessly laid on the hot stove top. The handle was designed to enable one to lift the lids safely without getting scorched by a hot stove. Mother still needed the tool when the stove was cold because the lids were heavy and lay flush with the stovetop. She inserted the end of this tool into the notch, lifted the lid and set it atop another lid. Into this opening she emptied two or three scoops of coal to fire the stove. Dad saved plane-shavings and ends of lumber from his carpentry projects for Mother to use as kindling. To start the fire she also put in some scraps of newspaper before Dad had a chance to read it (actually, she did not dare chance that).

To the left of the stove, from a nail on the wall, hung a metal match holder, always there— a kitchen necessity. We kept it adequately filled with strike-anywhere matches. To light the stove, Mother took a match, struck it on the rough metal stovetop (I guess that qualified as "anywhere"). She dropped the

lighted match onto the kindling, then replaced the lid. We used bituminous (soft) coal, surface mined and plentiful in Ohio (hence, cheap). The stove fired and heated up quickly, thus cooking ensued within minutes.

An omnipresent stovetop duo was a blue and white speckled graniteware coffee pot and a cast-iron tea kettle.

A stovepipe led to the chimney to draw off carbon monoxide and other noxious gasses (formed during coal combustion in the stove and furnace alike).

In the corner between the stove and chimney stood a small icebox. It was made of— what else? Oak. It held fresh dairy products (milk and cream) and not much else. It stood about four foot high with doors on the front—two small upper doors and a large lower one. Tin sheets lining these compartments served as insulation. Weekly during the summer, "The Iceman Cameth" to bring us a big block of ice, about eight inches square, maybe a foot long. The ice block loaded neatly into a fourth compartment up top by means of a hinged lid. The three food compartments loaded from the front. The small upper compartments held butter and schmearkase; the lower, taller compartment held milk and cream in glass quart jars. We did not store vegetables, fruits, meat or eggs in the icebox. It was truly a "box for ice" and I don't recall our family ever having a refrigerator when I was growing up.

A drain tube carried water away from the top compartment as the ice melted. The water drained into a pan that sat on the floor underneath the icebox. A hinged flap in front (just off the floor) lifted for ease of access to the drain pan so it could be emptied. When the overflowing pan peed a puddle on the floor, we knew it was time to empty it. The pan seemed always to overflow-- exactly why the linoleum around the icebox always appeared to be the cleanest and buckled the quickest.

In winter, we didn't spend money on ice. We could go down to the creek and get some ice. Milk was kept cold on the back stoop or kept cool in the basement. We had fresh eggs every day and used so many there was no time (or need) to refrigerate them. (Eggs, if never refrigerated, keep for weeks. Eggs, once refrigerated, must be kept cold to prevent spoilage.)

O THERWISE-- WINTER OR SUMMER-- WE HAD FEW MEANS TO HANDLE FOOD: WE HAD TO EAT IT, CAN IT, CURE IT, DRY IT, FERMENT IT, PICKLE IT OR STORE IT IN THE FRUIT CELLAR.

Mother kept a set of three nested earthenware mixing bowls on top of the icebox.

Half of the chimney in the downstairs extended into the living room and the other half was in the kitchen on the west wall. To its left ran the clothes chute, passing through from upstairs *en route* to the basement. The door to the clothes chute was made of old pine and swung open to the left. The chute was convenient for tossing in soiled tablecloths or hand towels, sparing someone a round-trip down cellar. We kids were always spilling milk onto the tablecloth, so the clothes chute was a blessing.

Still in the kitchen-- next to the chimney, on the right, were the entryways into the living room and cellar, respectively. The cellar door opened to the left (favoring as usual right-handed operators). On the north wall, between the cellar door (to the left) and where the stairs went up (to the right) was the kitchen sink console with its complement of drawers and cupboards. This sink-storage complex was affixed onto the stairwell encasement enclosing our home's two stairways.

A small white porcelain sink sat at the far right of this console. It had one basin. A built-in porcelain drain board occupied the counter space to the left of the sink. Notably, Mother had no open counter space because of this arrangement. There was no counter space in the kitchen whatsoever. Above, to the left of and beneath the sink was a **L**-shaped storage space. Above the drain board and sink was a bank of cupboards. There, we stored bowls, cups, glasses, pitchers and plates. To the left of the sink and drain board was another bank of cupboards above and a trio of drawers below.

*T*HE UPPERMOST CUPBOARD TO THE LEFT HELD SPICES, COCOA, HONEY AND OTHER BAKING SUPPLIES APPLIED TO NAUSEATING KITCHEN EXPERIMENTS OF CHILDHOOD.

Below the spice cupboard, we kept silverware in the top drawer. Beneath the silverware drawer was a capacious drawer about a foot high, for storing aprons, hand towels and tablecloths. The lowest drawer was also big and held pans, pots and tools (such as potato mashers and ladles). Completing the ⌐-shaped console-- the storage area below the sink held cleaning supplies, including lye (a commodity to be respected). We used lye to soften up the hard water from our well when washing dishes. We kept a pig bucket for food scraps and soured milk in the storage area under the drain board.

None of the kitchen cupboards had doors. The one below the sink had a piece of ordinary cotton cloth suspended from a string to conceal the pig bucket (from the eyes but not from the nose) and cleaning supplies.

What a chore to wash, dry and stow the dishes and utensils a family of seven or eight dirtied during a meal.

ROUNDING OUT THE KITCHEN, AT ITS NORTHEAST CORNER, STOOD A PROUD BUFFET WHERE WE STORED EXTRA LINENS, LARGE POTS AND PANS, AND "GOOD" PLATES RESERVED FOR COMPANY THAT DIDN'T FIT IN THE CUPBOARDS (THAT'S WHERE WE SHOULD HAVE PUT THE COMPANY: IN THE CUPBOARDS). BULKY ITEMS NOT FIT FOR THE CUPBOARDS (ROASTING PANS, SERVING DISHES, PLATTERS) WERE STORED IN, OR ON TOP OF, THE BUFFET. THE BUFFET VIED WITH THE STOVE AS TO WHICH WAS THE BIGGER AND MORE INVALUABLE PIECE OF EQUIPMENT.

Our kitchen floor was a single sheet of multicolored linoleum in greens, red and blues. Its surface cracked and curled at the doorways and under the ice box. Dad patched it periodically and had to replace the entire sheet eventually. (When was the handy, square linoleum tile invented? Linoleum *per se* was patented c. 1860.)

In the summer, coils of flypaper hung from the ceiling and twirled in a breeze. We had no screens in the windows but we had a screen door. How much sense does that make! The screen frequently needed to be replaced because we kids pushed on the mesh instead of on the door proper. We had no ceiling fan— or any other kind of fans. We had to accept the summer heat. Our only air conditioning was via an open window with a stiff breeze, if that. But we were used to it. Opening the two kitchen windows and leaving the back door open (with the screen door closed) didn't help much.

---

"**D**ON'T <u>SLAM</u> THE SCREEN DOOR!" MOTHER SAID ALL SUMMER LONG, TO SIX OR SEVEN PAIRS OF DEAF EARS.
WE SLAMMED THE DOOR ANYWAY.
SHE WAS ALWAYS— ALWAYS— SAYING THAT.
"DON'T SLA-AM THE SCREEN DOOR!"

---

Such was the kitchen, a much lived-in place. The tour of the downstairs is complete.

# VIGNETTE: TOM'S ONE LIFE.

WE WERE NEVER ALLOWED TO HAVE PETS IN THE HOUSE. WE HAD TWO DOGS, LAEG AND SKIPPY, BUT THEY LIVED OUTDOORS. WE HAD CATS IN THE BARN. IN GENERAL, WE DID NOT LOOK UPON DOGS AND CATS AS HOUSE PETS. BUT ONE TIME, A BLACK CAT WHICH HUNG AROUND THE YARD AND WHOM WE HAD NAMED TOMMY, GOT INTO THE HOUSE, WENT INTO THE CLOSET OFF OF DAD'S OFFICE AND WENT NUMBER TWO IN ONE OF DODIE'S "GOOD" SHOES. SHE WAS FURIOUS AT THE DISCOVERY. POOR TOMMY WAS BANISHED FROM THE HOUSE. THE REST OF US HAD A GOOD LAUGH AT DODIE'S EXPENSE FOR QUITE SOME TIME.

TOMMY HAD HIS ONE CHANCE AND HE BLEW IT.

--C. 1935

# CHAPTER 6:
## EARLY ENTERTAINMENT.

*THAT ROMAN CATHOLIC PRIEST WAS CANADIAN. THE PREJUCRIT NEVER CONVERTED ANY OF US.*

SUPPER time was 6:00 on the dot. After the table was cleared (even before the table was cleared) all of us piled into the living room to affix ourselves to the radio. One of us younger girls stayed behind in the kitchen to dry dishes as Mother washed-- whoever was the designated dish dryer of the day. This unfortunate kid had to crane an ear to catch as much of the radio program as the din from slopping dishwater and clinking dishes allowed.

We only had the one radio--- the RCA Victor.

MOTHER ACQUIRED A SECOND RADIO, FOR THE KITCHEN, DURING WORLD WAR II, TO LISTEN TO KDKA AS SHE WORKED.

Radio was to us what television and the computer would become to future generations.

We drew our chairs around the radio like cowboys hunkered around a campfire. While Mother did the dishes, Homer and I *squarshed* into her black rocker. When she came in the living room after ridding up the kitchen, we sprang up to allow Mother to get off her feet.

We all gave the radio our undivided attention.

I recall listening in the afternoon to "Jack Armstrong, the All-American Boy." This show hawked advertisements for magic rings and secret-code rings. We were allowed to send for some of them.

One of our favorites was "Amos 'n' Andy," a show about two black friends (portrayed by two white men). We thought their show was funny and the two men performed dozens of different, distinct character voices.

Another show was "The Jack Benny Program" (Jack, originally Benjamin Kubelsky of Chicago) who aired along with his real-life wife, Mary Livingstone; and Jack's valet, Rochester— who always called Jack, "boss." These two programs, broadcast Sunday evenings, were the highlight of our week. My family thought both shows were hilarious. We also heard news bulletins— I recall especially Lowell Thomas's news program. We were all working or attending school during the day— so I don't know any programs broadcast earlier in the day, that is, if radio shows were broadcast during the day then (early radio was not aired 24 hours a day or all night long, as nowadays).

We all went to bed at 9 or 10 at night.

A lot of religious programs were offered. One preacher was Father Coughlin, a Catholic priest from Canada. He was awful. His irreligious spoutings scared me and Homer.

FATHER COUGHLIN WAS RAVING AGAINST SIN. AND AGAINST THE GOVERNMENT SPENDING OF MONEY. COME TO THINK OF IT—AREN'T THOSE BOTH THE SAME?

He was a menace: a prejudice and a hypocrite, i.e., a "prejucrite." He set out to inflame the public. And it was totally scary. Totally *total*. He was vicious. No need to give him any more air time here for he was so awful.

He never converted any of us.

Speaking of converting-- instead of frittering away her time listening to the radio or playing cards, Elaine should have been have been practicing her right-handed penmanship. Our teacher was engaged in an ambitious (however futile) campaign to convert Elaine away from a southpaw's wicked ways. But Elaine was so indignant at the very idea, she wasn't (practicing or converting).

We always listened to fights on the radio. Oh, yeah! We listened to bouts involving Max Schmeling, Max Baer Sr., Joe Louis— he was called the "Brown Bomber"-- and James J. Braddock, whom we called Jimmy.

On Thursdays, at 6:30 p.m., Mother and Dad left for the Lodge Hall in Berlin Center. Byron belonged to the Knights of Pythias and Blanche to the Order's auxiliary, the Pythian Sisters. We always wondered what in the world they did up there, but information from that quarter was not forthcoming. The Pythians kept their organization more secret than the codes on Jack Armstrong's rings.

While my parents were at Lodge, Doris, Delmus, Elaine and I squeezed around the floor register in the living room to play cards. We were hoping to catch some heat coming up from the furnace. We played 500 and that was it. We never played any other card game. And I don't even know how to play it today, although I know the Joker had a lot to do with 500. We did not wait up for Mother and Dad to come home from Lodge—we went to bed early.

For additional entertainment, what a pleasure to take a chair out to the front porch on a warm summer day to read The Saturday Evening Post for its serial articles. The cover of the Post, often done up by Norman Rockwell, delighted all of us-- a special delight. Another publication we read on the front porch was Grit, a weekly, catchall newspaper with a store of knowledge and good advice—a sort of Benjamin Franklin in print. Speaking of Normal Rockwell— the walls of our house were bare—no framed paintings or photographs. The only wall-hanging was the calendar beside Dad's desk.

The steps of the porch faced south and led to the driveway. We didn't have any sidewalks.

# VIGNETTE: VINEGAR PUNCH.

WE KIDS HAD PERFECTED A RELIEF FOR HAVING EATEN TOO MUCH AT A FAMILY REUNION. OR WE MAKE IT OLD TIME WE FELT LIKE IT. WE DIDN'T NEED THE EXCUSE OF HAVING AN ACID STOMACH. FOR ENTERTAINMENT, WE FIXED A CONCOCTION THAT BROUGHT RELIEF OR AMUSEMENT OR BOTH. WE FILLED A GLASS THREE- QUARTERS WITH WATER, ADDED A SPLOSH OF VINEGAR AND A TEASPOONFUL OF SUGAR. WE THEN LEANED OVER THE SINK AND ADDED A TEASPOON OF BAKING SODA AND DRANK IT QUICKLY WHILE IT FIZZED. IT SPARKLED AND POPPED IN OUR FACES AND TICKLED OUR NOSES BUT IT TASTED SO GOOD. IT RELIEVED ANY FEELINGS OF DISCOMFORT.

WE CALLED THIS RELIEF A "VINEGAR PUNCH." WE MADE IT ANY TIME THE MOOD STRUCK-- WE MADE IT ESPECIALLY IF WE WERE JUST BORED.

--C. 1933

# CHAPTER 7:
## THE UPSTAIRS.

*"...I'M NOT ALWAYS RIGHT
BUT I'M NEVER WRONG..."*

*t*HE entrance to the second-floor stairway was in the northeast corner of the kitchen adjacent to the buffet. Its attractive door was the same type as every other door in the entire house (except the bathroom door, which was white and much smaller). These doors were varnished, paneled wood.

The first set of steps, 11 in all, led to a landing. This was convenient for storing dry goods: flour, rice and sugar that came in 50-pound sacks. We purchased salt in 25-pound bags.

A window in the landing (right above its counterpart, the cellar door leading outside, downstairs) looked out over the side yard. From here, we could see clearly, to the north, the corner of Western Reserve Road at Route 534. The window's central, clear pane was surrounded by four-inch-square panes of solid red, yellow, blue and green stained glass that always reminded me of Mother's colorful, translucent jellies and jams.

At one time, Mother's sewing machine also sat up there in the upstairs landing. We moved it into Dad's room around 1933 for her convenience and warmth— eliminating a trip upstairs every time Mother wanted to mend something. The landing was cold, so we keep the door on the first floor shut during winter to prevent cold air from drafting down into the kitchen.

From the landing three steps led up to the second floor— equivalent to the three cellar-landing steps directly beneath. To the right of the second step there (on the west side of the stairway) was access to the attic. It was not a true "attic" but a long crawl space occupying the house's northwest part. (The crawl space corresponded to the space occupied by the stairwell on the northeast part.) The attic was accessed through a panel (not a true door) about four foot high by three foot wide with a spring-latch closure. It opened to the left of course— otherwise the act of opening it would have knocked one off the steps. The crawl space was diminished by the slope of the roof. As with cobblers' kids who went shoeless, my dad-the-carpenter stored broken furniture in there and household odds and ends that he might have repaired otherwise.

At the top of this trio of little steps the hall entryway was an open, doorless space. Along the hallway, were three doors to the bedrooms: on the right, my parents' bedroom; on the left, the girls' bedrooms; beyond, the chimney and clothes chute, on the right (here, the chimney came up to emerge out the center of the roof). Straight ahead at the end of the hall was my brothers' bedroom door.

The first object-of-greeting upstairs was the bucket. It was the first thing seen (or sniffed). Suffice to say it was smelly. Right there on the floor, in plain view, this *pièce de résistance* welcomed royalty and commoner alike. Nestled awaitingly into the cove formed by the chimney's jutting into the hallway was this ordinary, two-and-a-half gallon scrub bucket. It was made of galvanized steel and had a wire handle. For obvious reasons, we kept the bucket covered with a rag.

*T*O US, THE BUCKET WAS A WELCOME RELIEF. IT SERVED FAITHFULLY AS OUR INDOOR TOILET FOR YEARS, A BETTER TWIN TO THE ASH BUCKET DOWN CELLAR. ON A FRIGID WINTER NIGHT, WHAT A FLAT-OUT BLESSING— IMAGINE THE INCONVENIENCE OF SPRINTING TO THE OUTHOUSE THROUGH THE SNOW FOR RELIEF.

Each morning, one of us had to empty the bucket. Here was an incentive to get dressed and downstairs quickly: this chore fell to the last person to come downstairs— and woe unto anyone who fell downstairs while doing it. We disposed of the mixed contents by heading out the back door, down to a drainage ditch Dad had dug. The ditch ended on the other side of the driveway at the bottom of the hill (leading up to the barn). Here we flung the slurry wide into the pasture— thankfully no one popped by for a visit at that early hour.

The grass out there was always greener. "The doo was cast." How offal. The bearer rinsed out the bucket at the outdoor spicket on the northeast corner of the house and returned the bucket to its proper place upstairs.

In the upstairs hallway, on the port side of the chimney, that clever invention (the laundry chute) began as an open shaft. The opening there had no door. (We little kids were tempted often to climb in and slide down to the basement. Common sense prevailed and we never pulled a stunt like that.) The laundry chute was quite a nice detail for a house built in 1903.

These two humble but ultra-modern conveniences then—bucket and laundry chute—were positioned on either side of the chimney.

As said, my parents' bedroom was at the top of the stairs to the right and beyond that my brothers' room-- these two rooms and the hallway occupied the west half of the upstairs (with the attic). The girls' bedrooms took up the east half of the second floor.

The door to my parents' room swung open to the left; that is, from the hallway, the knob was on the right. (Each bedroom door opened into its respective bedroom.) Just inside the door, the chimney stood to the left— jutting into the room just as it jutted into the hallway. Between the chimney and door was a floor register. This delivered the only heat to the upstairs.

At night, when it was time to go to bed, Dad or my older brother banked the fire in the furnace. A liberal amount of coal was added with an eye to keeping the fire burning throughout the night-- wishful thinking.

Among the bedrooms, my folks' was spacious, measuring about 12 by 14 foot. The flooring was made of a rough pine board, as opposed to the nice oak flooring downstairs. Their double bed was made of substantial wood. The mattress was done up from what we knew as "straw tick"— blue-and-white striped heavy cotton ticking, stuffed with clean straw from the barn storage. The pillows were filled with wads of cotton batting. Mother made our bed sheets by sewing sugar sacks and other fabrics together. Several quilts made by her hand completed the bedding.

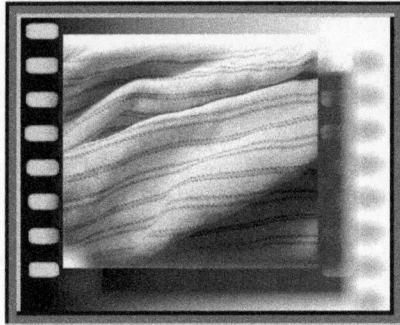

Mother claimed a chest of drawers as her own. This held her skirts, stockings, corsets, handkerchiefs and various mementos (old letters and postcards). On top of this chest was a white porcelain bowl and pitcher to serve Mother in her *toilette*. The chest was a bulky piece of furniture, with two side-by-side drawers at the top and two large drawers beneath those. The chest was made of rich, dark walnut.

Dad's dresser stood against the west wall. Smaller than Mother's chest of drawers, Dad's dresser had four drawers. Here Dad kept his handkerchiefs, shirts, socks and underwear. On the top of his dresser at night Dad laid out his old-standby pocketknife, pocket watch, pipe and tobacco, wallet and coins. There were two straight-backed chairs in their room. Two windows on the west wall overlooked the front lawn. The walls (as always) were painted white. The room had no wall-to-wall carpeting, merely a throw rug on either side of the bed. From the ceiling hung a simple pull-string light. The plastered ceiling angled according to the slant of the roof. The north wall of their bedroom was truncated where it abutted the attic.

Unique to my folks' bedroom was a walk-in closet in the southwest corner. The closet ran along the entire length of the south side of their room and opened into my brothers' room at the other end. This capacious closet was finished-out with plastered walls. From a sturdy dowel hung many wool suits my father's younger brother, Emerson, had handed down (rather, up) to Dad. Dad's shirts hung there, as did Mother's garments, including her favored "good" white dress she wore for special Lodge occasions. Hanging from a nail in the sloped ceiling was a holster with a Colt .45, a relic from the Great War. We children were fascinated by the long barrel on this service revolver. A favorite intrigue involved gazing at this formidable weapon without touching it-- we kids were forbidden to touch it and we never did. At the opposite end (in the east wall of the closet) was the door leading into my brothers' dormer-bedroom. The boys' clothes hung in that end. All four closet sharers kept their shoes on the floor.

The dormer room was accessed by this closet door on its west wall and its other (main) door stood past the chimney, at the end of the hallway. The dormer, visible from the road, was part of the original house construction. It rendered our house quite attractive.

A dormer (from the Latin, *to sleep*) with windows provides headroom in a roof space, light and ventilation for a house's upper floor. Dormers decoratively break up a roofline by protruding straight up through the plane of a sloped roof. Large dormers doubled as spare bedrooms in homes without requiring the expensive addition of a third floor. Without that extra bedroom, my brothers would have been out of luck—many children in families slept in make-shift cots in living rooms or basements. Our dormer room was a nine-foot-square postage stamp (barely room for a double bed and a dresser-- no chair-- no place in there for any business other than sleeping). The bed was pushed against the pair of windows. Only a foot of space remained to access the closet door, which (fortunately) opened into the closet (there was no room for that door to open into the boys' bedroom). The windows overlooked the driveway. Not even two feet separated the foot of the bed from the small three-drawer dresser that stood against the east wall.

Delmus enjoyed this sanctuary all to himself until Homer was old enough to sleep in a big bed. Until then, my older brother was the only family member with a private bedroom. What luxury.

The rooms opposite my parents' bedroom belonged to us girls. The east half of the upstairs floor plan was originally one open space. My dad framed out two smaller bedrooms by building a thin partition of lath and plaster up to the ceiling and, afterwards, installing a door. One needed to walk through the room off the hallway to enter the second. Elaine and I shared the north bedroom. The older girls, Flo and Dodie, took the south one. This precluded our privacy, Elaine's and mine. Our older sisters awakened us by tip-toeing in from late-night dates or tip-toeing out to the bucket, at odd hours.

In June 1935, when Flo left to be married, another private room opened up. The next-in-line inherited this privilege—Doris had it to herself then and lorded it over both of us little squirts.

There were no closets in either girls' bedroom. Delmus put up rods for us in the northwest corner of each room, where we hung blouses and sweaters.

> *I*N MY ROOM, A SMALL WASHSTAND WITH DRAWERS HELD OUR SOCKS AND UNDERS. THE OLDER GIRLS' ROOM HAD A DRESSER WITH THREE DRAWERS FOR THEIR DRAWERS.

Both rooms held a double, cast-iron bed, painted white. The mattresses were not "mattresses" at all, but straw-filled ticking laid atop flimsy bedsprings. A periodic trip to the barn to replenish the filling—allowed one night of bliss on fluffy, new straw. The straw in the ticks crushed up and disintegrated fast.

A window in each room faced the hill leading up to the barnyard and to the laying house.

Elaine had overnight guests often, putting us three abed. Elaine and this girl always stuck me in the middle.

I never thought of it this way before, but what we always called the "upstairs" was not truly a full second story. Instead, our house was one story (with a basement) that had bedrooms in what was effectively the attic. It makes sense looking at it this way-- certainly explains what it was like up there in the winter: we froze. No attic or crawl space created a buffer of air above the bedrooms to ameliorate the cold. The roof doubled as the ceiling. Immediately beyond was the cold, grey Ohio sky.

Grab the bucket— you're the last one upstairs. Head out the back door, downstairs.

"And don't slam the screen door!"

And please don't trip and spill the slop bucket!

*** 

Downstairs, the back door led to a porch with a plain railing, which was functional, not decorative. The back porch did not extend the entire length of the east side of the house. It started at the window near the buffet and ended in a set of steps just beyond the bathroom window. The steps led directly to the drive and, immediately beyond that, the garage. Mom's plants lined the back-porch railing in summer but she left us room to perch as we chattered with an occasional visitor. We never sat on the back porch to read a book or magazine.

The front porch faced four maple trees in the front yard and Route 534 beyond. About 1930, Dad built a sturdier banister rail around the front porch, as it was a good place for leisure. Waiting for the mailman, the newspaper delivery man, the grocery truck or simply watching for Dad to return from an errand was an enjoyable pastime. What a pleasure to haul a chair out to the front porch to read a magazine.

The front porch steps were made of cement. We congregated there just for fun.

"Don't sit on the steps," Mother said. "You'll get piles." Of course we never did get piles.

We spent hours talking on the front porch, sitting on the railing. Dad made this railing wider than the one he built on the back porch. (Recent photographs reveal the rail is gone now from the front porch.) Perhaps after years of ice, rain and snow, wood rot set in and the banister was removed.

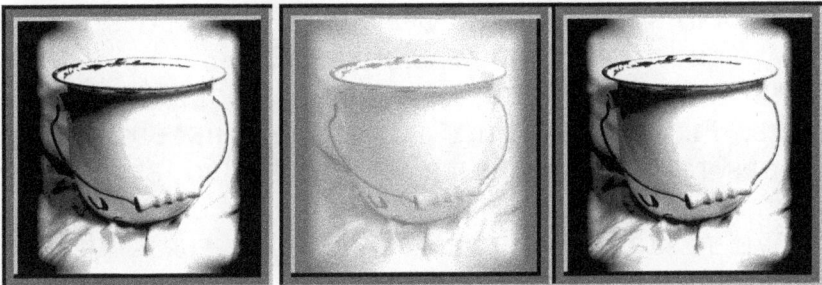

What I would give for one more chance to walk into that house and sit on the stool next to the stove and watch my dear, sweet mother tending to her bread-baking.

# VIGNETTE: BOWL HAIRCUTS.

BEFORE LEAVING HOME TO ATTEND KENT STATE NORMAL SCHOOL, FLO WAS A TREMENDOUS HELP TO MOTHER IN RAISING US. MY PARENTS DIDN'T TAKE US UP TO THE BARBER SHOP FOR HAIR CUTS. THEY COULDN'T SPARE THE EXPENSE OR THE TIME TO RUN US UP TO BERLIN CENTER. HAIRCUTS AT HOME WERE CONVENIENT AND FREE. LIKE MANY A TASK, IT FELL TO FLORENCE. SHE WAS THE OLDEST AND HAD A LITTLE FLAIR WITH THE SCISSORS. STILL HARD TO BELIEVE WHEN I WAS 6, FLO WAS 20.

FOR THOSE MEMORABLE— WRETCHED! -- HAIRCUTS, ONE OF US SAT ON THE KITCHEN STOOL. FLO SECURED A SUGAR-SACK TOWEL AROUND THE VICTIM'S NECK WITH A SAFETY PIN. SHE PLACED A MIXING BOWL UPSIDE DOWN ON TOP OF AN UNRULY MOP OF HAIR AND SIMPLY SNIPPED OFF THE FRINGE THAT STUCK OUT BENEATH THE EDGE. QUITE FASHIONABLE.

"SIT STILL!" SHE SAID, AS SOMEONE FIDGETED UNDER THE BLADES. FLO *THONKED* THE BOWL WITH THE BUTT OF THE SCISSORS TO GET A SQUIRMER TO QUIT CRYING, SETTLE DOWN AND SIT STILL. THIS ONLY MADE THE SQUIRMER CRY MORE.

WE REFERRED TO THESE LAVISH *COIFFURES* AS "BOWL HAIRCUTS." IT BECAME SUCH A FAMILY JOKE, HARD TO TELL NOW IF THOSE QUIRKY-SHAPED HAIRCUTS WERE REAL OR IMAGINED. IN A PHOTOGRAPH OF US SIX KIDS TAKEN IN 1927 (PAGE 123), OUR LITTLE CAMPBELL-SOUP-KIDS HAIRCUTS ARE PROOF ENOUGH OF OUR SUBJECTION TO THE BOWL. FLO IS THE ONLY ONE SPORTING A STYLED HAIRDO. MAKES ONE WONDER WHO DO'ED FLO'S DO.

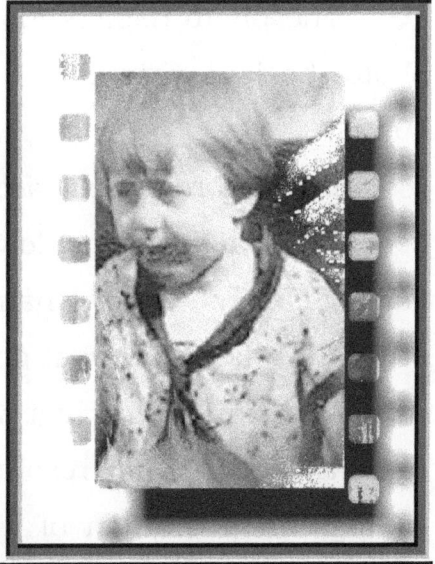

# CHAPTER 8.
## THE EARLY YEARS, 1924-1929.

*" SHUT YOUR MOUTH & EAT YOUR SUPPER. "*

--DAD

*a* COPY of a photograph from my family album shows us six children standing at the edge of my grandparents' front yard—at my mother's parents' place. Grandma and Grandpa Cline lived in Berlin Center a few houses north of the main intersection of State Routes 224 and 534.

The photo depicts Florence holding Homer. In the photo, he is 1 year old. The photograph was taken in 1927.

In the foreground, a child, age 3, with light blonde hair and straight bangs down to her eyebrows, sports the latest fashion: a bowl haircut. She is wearing a print dress that hangs straight down like her bangs. Her loose cotton stockings are just visible above the knee. The camera captured her resolutely marching away from her siblings on a mission of no small import— leaving her siblings in the dust.

The blonde little tot is yours truly.

At the time this photo was snapped, Elaine was 5; Doris, 8; and Flo, 17. My big brother, Delmus, was 11. This was an occasion of some sort—Delmus, for example, is dressed in a white shirt with a patterned tie, knickers and a flat cap. We were visiting my grandparents on a Sunday with all of us dressed in our best outfits— we never dressed up during the week. This photo neatly captures all six of us in our finery two years before the Depression hit.

I'd like to know what Elaine is holding in her right paw. Whatever it is, I am holding one in my left hand. Grandma Cline could have given us cookies. Even so, it wasn't sufficient to wipe a scowl off Elaine's face.

We younger girls are dressed so alike in this picture— here is concrete proof that my clothes were hand-me-downs.   (I had to wait 10 years before acquiring a new article of clothing, a jacket Dad ordered for me alone from Sears.)   Flo is wearing a stylish, homemade dress.   She holds Homer, whose attire seems to be in keeping with his age, all bundled up no matter the season.

Weren't we a fine-looking bunch?

Back to 1925. When I was a year old, Mother was pregnant again. She delivered Homer Howard on April 22, 1926. The last addition to the family, Homer was our baby brother. In the ensuing years, Homer proved to be my good friend and pal. Because of the proximity in our ages, we always played and shared secrets together.

In 1927, although I do not recall the event personally, we surely listened to famous radio broadcasts covering Charles Lindbergh's record-shattering flight across the Atlantic. His non-stop trip was the first of its kind. (I have seen a replica of his original plane, "Spirit of St. Louis," hanging in the lobby of the Lambert-St. Louis International Airport.) I can imagine our family sitting around the RCA Victor listening to that world-shaking news— talked about for years.

My first memory harks back to 1929—to an incident regarding Mother's health. (I was 5 years old and remember not one single prior event.) I distinctly recollect that Dad had to drive Mother to Youngstown to obtain a truss the doctor had ordered for her. Venturing to Youngstown was rare. Dad only made the trip for work, or for doctor or hospital visits.

All of us kids were left at home to wonder what was to become of my poor mother. She and Dad remained secretive about her condition. We only caught guarded mention of "a truss" and glimpses of the ugly apparatus, crafted from steel and leather, as it lay draped over the back of a chair in Mother's room as she rested in bed.

Could her injury have been caused by working so hard— leaning over, lifting heavy objects such as children, furniture, laundry baskets, buckets of coal or water-- a latent result of six childbirths or combinations of all? It was never made clear. Adults never discussed private matters with children. And my parents certainly never discussed such matters in front of or with any of us. Left on our own, we morbidly churned our own dark thoughts about the disposition of Mother's injury. For all we knew (or didn't know) — she might have been dying. We were left in ignorance, to fear the worst, to guess the true nature of her problem, which was likely an abdominal hernia.

My parents returned from Youngstown with the truss for Mother and gifts for all us kids. They brought Homer and me matching pairs of OshKosh B'Gosh bib overalls. They were cut from a smart, blue-and-white striped denim fabric. This matter of the truss became my first memory because of those overalls. They came as a complete surprise and more. This was my first pair of overalls. At age 3, Homer might still have been in diapers. What a notch up on the fashion scale for him! He and I were fascinated by all the pockets, especially on the bib. There were pockets for pencil stubs and pockets to store secret childhood treasures. On another layer, those overalls demonstrated affection in my parents' repertoire, for they were not physically demonstrative of affection. For my parents to spend money on gifts for us (even before the Great Depression) meant they were thinking of us while attending to Mother's injury. The overalls symbolized their love for us. We proudly wore them and wore them again until they just wore out. We wore our striped overalls for years until, one day, Mother pried us out of them and cut them up for rags.

Such is the first memory of my entire life: those OshKosh overalls, b'gosh.

From the age of 5 on, my memory is reliable. Two years later, Mother experienced another private matter. She needed an operation. Dad admitted her to Salem Hospital in 1931. Again, no one ever revealed the nature of the procedure to us. I know it was female in nature— probably a hysterectomy. It was hush-hush to the utmost. To this day I do not know for certain. Nothing was explained in any detail to us kids. We were instructed to keep quiet and to not disturb Mother in any fashion.

Dad, ever clever, invented a way to keep us from being underfoot while Mother healed, upstairs. He, with

Delmus helping out, constructed a mighty swing down in the pasture alongside the creek. The seat was two inches thick, about one foot by three foot long, made from two boards laid side by side along their lengths, with two end caps. Dad cut a **U**-shaped slot in the side of each end cap that abutted the boards. I'm not sure why he used four pieces of wood. Perhaps he didn't have an auger-bit large enough to drill a hole to accommodate the rope (odd, since he was a carpenter).

Dad and Delmus used extremely thick hemp rope — at least three inches in diameter. Two sections of rope were lashed around a sturdy tree limb high above. The nether end of each rope was passed through an end-cap slot, then stiffly knotted underneath. The tree was across the creek, in a copse among other old trees thriving long before Sumner Stanley came along. Stately walnut trees rose on the near side of the creek. On the far side were mammoth maples, willows and oaks; and chestnuts before disease wiped them out. The tree Dad picked for our swing was one of these majestic giants, whose substantial limb bore the pair of ropes. How Dad got those huge ropes up and over the limb of that tree and securely fastened I can only imagine, Maybe he made Delmus shimmy up there or rigged up a weight to throw them over. Dad could achieve the impossible so he somehow figured it out.

As a result we spent many hours down at our little creek, known universally as "the crick," wading in the water or playing on the wooden swing. The swing was so accommodating—we sat on it three abreast. In the crick, we amused ourselves by pulling the tails off innocent crawdads and kept a lookout for frogs and water snakes.

While my mother recuperated from her surgery, to whom did the task fall of preparing special meals for her-- baking and cooking for us, bathing us kids, laundering our clothes and caring for us in general?  Surely, once again, the responsibility must have fallen to Flo, who was 21 in 1931. Dad insisted that each of us help Flo. Certainly I, at age 7, and Homer, 5, were of little help.

The stock market crash of October 1929, affected us personally.  Throughout the Depression it was true— our family always had enough to eat.  We raised our own chickens and pigs for meat, produced fresh dairy products from our cow, and from our laying hens gathered eggs to eat or sell.  We tended a substantial kitchen garden.  But, hard to come by were commodities we couldn't produce, such as coats, gloves, galoshes, hats, shoes and socks; food we didn't produce, for example, cheese, bananas, citrus fruits or beef; school supplies like paper, pencils and books; and farm supplies, e.g., gasoline and chicken feed. All these we had to buy with cash that grew harder to come by as the Depression intensified.

We knew we were in a Depression because there was never any money for anything extra, beyond purchasing seeds for the garden, say, and feed for the chickens and other farm animals. Our neighbors talked about the Depression incessantly-- how hard times were.

Carpentry jobs grew scarce as the months of the Depression threatened to linger into years. My dad acquired the idea to work for himself as a poultry farmer. Roosevelt's Works Progress Administration crews swept through later, in 1933 and beyond. Dad had his pride. He consistently refused to work in the steel mills in Youngstown. He never accepted what he considered to be "welfare," for example, signing up for WPA work. By the time WPA came around, Dad had already taken the initiative to work for himself. When evident that he could no longer rely on carpentry jobs, Dad turned to something more consistent and closer to home: raising chickens professionally.

Before 1929, when Dad worked fulltime as a carpenter, we tended about 10 chickens that were more like family pets than wage earners. Our little handful of chickens provided us with sufficient eggs for us along and no one else. About 1930 or 1931, Dad hit upon an ingenious idea. I do not know if someone suggested this, if it were Mother's idea or a B.-E.-Woolf original. Still, this idea established "Willow Run Farm." Our poultry operation thus expanded exponentially from simply gathering eggs for our own table from our pets, to providing a surfeit of eggs for profit. Dad expanded our farm so we could accommodate more laying hens-- up to about 300 by 1935 and *beaking* at about 1,500 lay-ers (laying hens) toward 1942.

In 1937, Dad added another facet to this operation that increased our family income dramatically— he quit buying baby chicks from New Jersey and, instead, installed incubators that allowed us to hatch our own baby chicks. Three-fourths of these chicks we set aside to expand our own poultry operation and the remaining fourth we sold to local farmers. This income augmented the cash we generated from selling eggs to a local egg cooperative.

Herein lay the genius: all our neighbors were dairy farmers. They raised cows and wholesaled their milk through a middleman just as we did. They had their own dairy cooperative that turned around and re-sold milk to hotels, restaurants, grocery stores and other retail outlets at a greater profit. Our corner of northeast Ohio was largely settled by proud German and English immigrants. Their progeny raised Jersey or Holstein cattle, not chickens. That was the picture. Our one or two dairy cows fed our family so we did not need to buy butter, cheese or whole milk from them but they turned around and bought eggs and pullets (young laying hens) from us.

We had a good one-way thing going. No other poultry farms in our area existed. Our own *Money-opoly* of sorts (Monopoly, the game, was patented in 1935).

Mother was allowed to keep the money she made from selling eggs (with cracked shells) to neighbors (cracked and otherwise). With her egg money, she bought little gifts and treats for us children, penny candy and such-- a special act. Mother never thought of herself first.

# VIGNETTE: POLE VAULTING.

I N THE SPRING WHEN THE RAINS CAME HOMER AND I FETCHED A LONG STURDY POLE WHICH WE CALLED A "VAULTING POLE." WE SKIPPED DOWN TO THE CRICK AND FOLLOWED IT CLEAR DOWN UNTIL IT CAME OUT AT WESTERN RESERVE ROAD. SOMETIMES WE FELL IN THE RUSHING WATER AND HAD TO RETURN HOME EARLY FROM OUR SURVEYS. WE HAD FUN STICKING THE POLE IN TO THE MIDDLE OF THE CRICK AND VAULTING ACROSS TO THE OTHER SIDE. WE HAD TO GET THE POLE RIGHT IN THE MIDDLE TO AVOID FALLING IN. WE WENT HOME WET AND TIRED AND EXHILERATED. IT WAS REALLY FUN.

–C. 1933

# THE MILL CREEK SCHOOL YEARS: 1930-1935.

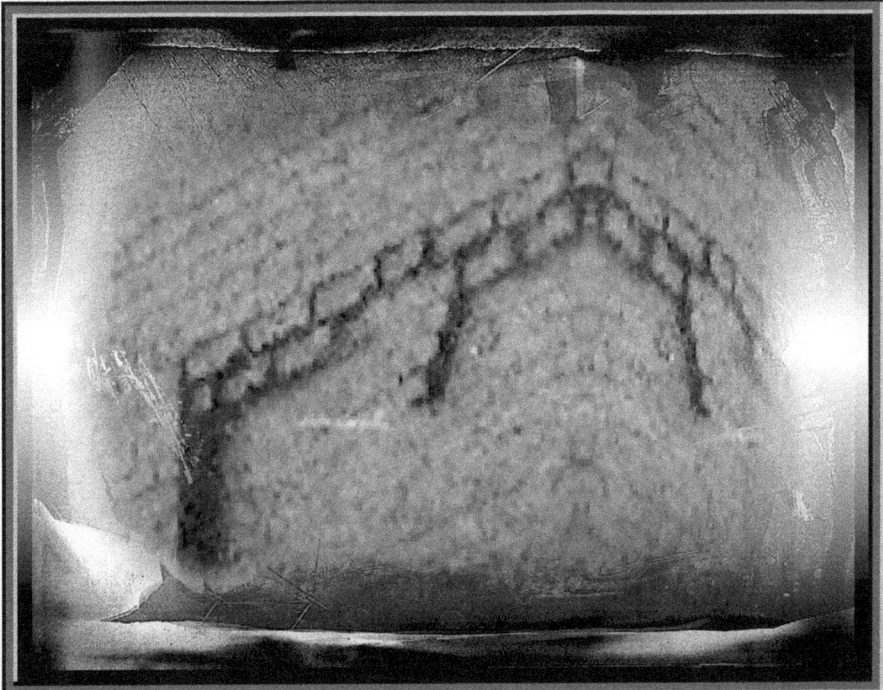

# CHAPTER 9:
## THE SCHOOLHOUSE.

*...WITHOUT FURTHER ADON'T...*

--JLG

STARTED school in 1930 when I was 6. Elaine and Doris were already there— in third and sixth grade, respectively. Our school provided for grades one through six, so '30 was Doris's last year there.

A mile from our home, the schoolhouse was on Calla Road just a short distance east of Route 534. Locals called this intersection "Boyd's Corner" because the north-west corner was owned by a semi-profitable farmer, Bob Boyd. He was a hard-scrabble, rather ruthless fellow who had his hand in about 20 quasi-farm-related enterprises (some of them shady). Farming was his main source of income.

He was cruel to animals.

School started at 9 a.m. and let out at 3 p.m. on the dot. We walked both ways. (I was in the fifth grade when school busses started that particular run.) Doris and Elaine set out for school, with me in tow. How, at age 6, my spindly legs carried me the mile to school and back, I do not know. We left our books at school, sparing us the burden of lugging them to-and-fro. We did carry our lunches, wrapped up in newspaper (hopefully ones my dad had already read). I probably lagged behind Elaine and Doris the entire mile. The round-trip was uphill both ways— especially in winter, through six-foot snow drifts in the wind in the summer... Hold on—we didn't go to school in summer!

We had to walk on the side of the road, as there were no sidewalks. We stayed on the east side— not for safety, but because we lived on that side, so no need to cross the highway. ("Walk on Left, Face Approaching Traffic" was a State safety slogan that came later.) When we got to Boyd's Corner, we crossed Calla Road, turned left and walked on the south side of the road, a short 100 yards to the schoolhouse.

My formal education began there, in this endearing one-room schoolhouse, "Mill Creek School." Additionally, three other identical one-room schools were strategically located in Goshen Township, to accommodate farm children just like us. Boswell, Patmos and Goshen Center were these other elementary schools.

Flo might have taught me to read, to learn the alphabet before I started school and to write my name, for I arrived the first day already knowing how to read and write. With no preschool or kindergarten, farm families that had the wherewithal taught the rudiments to their offspring before sending them off to grade school.

Mill Creek School was held in a substantial, dark-red-brick building built to last. Its steeply pitched, light-gray slate roof had a belfry. The little brook, Mill Creek that ran through this area, imparted its name to our school. The site occupied about three-fourths of an acre. In addition to our school *per se*, the site housed an attached coal shed on the west side and two privies in the side yard to the east (one for girls, one for boys). The privies were ramshackle affairs that could have been tipped over easily. Not built atop a deep hole, they just stood atop the ground, instead, and got mucked out from the rear (so to speak) by a workman who threw in lime after cleaning it out. (Lime cut down the odor and kept flies away.) The privies were cold and drafty in winter.

The Township chose a parcel of land irregular in contour for Mill Creek School. To say the least, it was unsuitable for the plow. The schoolhouse sat on a flattened foundation. A five-foot-deep drainage ditch ran parallel to Calla Road at the front. The land sloped slightly downward toward 534 to the west of the school. On the east, a steep slope ran down away from the school to the privies and the fence beyond. Behind the school to the south it was the exact opposite— the land sloped upward to a degree that made it difficult to play games. A poor choice of terrain as a playscape for gradeschool kids. Let's trust that the Township Trustees got this land at a bargain price, as it surely made an even poorer choice for farmland to whichever farmer sold it off.

The belfry atop the school stood directly above the stoop. Our teacher rang the belfry's large bell to signal the end of recess, though we didn't have far to roam from the front door. (The building had only one door but we called it the "front door.") No emergency exit was provided for the schoolhouse that, when fully occupied, housed about 18 students plus one teacher.

The school was set back not more than 30 feet from Calla Road, which the door faced. A huge stone step was situated in front of the door. Standing on that step with the door to your back, you'd be facing north.

On sunny days, we schoolkids sat on the stone step during lunch break. We huddled under the covered stoop on rainy days or remained indoors. A dirt path led to the driveway on the west side of the school, where one might have seen a flivver (Ford Model T car) parked there.

The schoolhouse interior was spacious, especially as seen through the eyes of a first grader-- truly one room with no partitions or walls of any kind to divide the space into grades. Demarcation of grades was accomplished simply by the seating arrangement of the desks.

*T*HE DESIGN OF THE SCHOOL'S INTERIOR WAS ELEMENTARY AND— AS SOON ENOUGH TO BE REVEALED— COMPLETELY

Backwards

The door (the front door) was made of heavy wood, with no windows. It opened inward and swung to the left, again favoring the right-hander from the outside. Inside, to the right was a huge, round furnace that sat about six feet out from the north and west walls. We were able to walk completely around the furnace. Near the furnace, the rope for the school bell came down through the ceiling. Even though the furnace was in the front of the building, we deemed it to be in the back because when we were seated at our desks facing the south wall (which was actually the back of the building) the furnace was at our backs.

I'll let you figure that one out!

The coal-fired furnace warmed up the northwest corner cozily but barely heated the rest of the interior. The cast-iron furnace, sheathed with a light grey metal for decoration and insulation, frequently needed to be stoked with fist-sized chunks of fuel. The loading door was situated conveniently on the east portion of the furnace and another door beneath that allowed for ash removal.

Coal was stored in the wooden shed on the west side of the schoolhouse. The coal man had a chute that fit on the back of his dump truck. He raised the bed and large, dusty chunks of coal fell through the top of the coalhouse's open lid. (He was not the same coal man who delivered coal to our house.) The coal came from a storage yard in Garfield, Ohio, south on Route 534. The coal was not strip-mined there, but shipped in by rail.

At school, the older boys were expected to carry in coal to fire the furnace. Girls were not required to haul coal when boys were present. There was always a bucket full of coal sitting there next to the furnace, awaiting the next stoking.

The opposite side of the north wall hosted a row of black cast-iron coat hooks, east of the door. The hooks were fairly low, perhaps, four feet off the floor. Here we hung our coats, stocking hats, mittens and scarves. Our boots were lined up on the floor beneath. Wet boots made the floor sloppy. Next came a single window. The windows in our schoolhouse were unusually tall, about 10 foot high. For a 6-year-old kid to look up at a 10-foot window—well, they seemed huge. Then came built-in shelves for school supplies: crêpe paper, pencils, poster board, spare books and our lunches.

The east wall was graced by four windows. In warm months, we were allowed to open these screenless windows. During the winter, that was a cold wall to have to sit by, for the upper graders. The fifth and sixth graders sat as far away from the furnace as possible-- dictated by the floor plan. Between the windows were two pictures, which I can still see in my mind's eye. They have stayed with me over the many years. The photograph on the right side of the fourth window was of the majestic cathedral at Rheims, France (a site I visited half a century later). The picture to the left of the fourth window was of Frances Willard, a beloved educator-turned-suffragist and advocate for temperance during the late 1800's. In her photo, she watched over us students with what seemed a stern demeanor (in the judgment of a 6-year-old). There were only two pictures hanging in the entire school (one has to wonder about the interior decorator) --one, a building, the other, a person (Miss Willard). She influenced the enactment of the 18th Amendment to the Constitution, the Volstead Act (banning alcohol manufacture, transport and sale-- created Prohibition, 1920 to 1933). Who knows? When this batty law was passed, Miss Willard and her cronies might have celebrated at a local pub with a round of Scotch whiskey.

The windowless south wall hosted three blackboards, each six foot square with a little tray for erasers and for white chalk the thickness of a little finger.

Centered on this back wall was a 6-by-10 foot wooden stage, elevated approximately eight inches. The teacher's plain oak desk sat center stage, with a straight-backed wooden chair and wastepaper basket and not much more.

If there were a dunce's stool I do not recall one. On the other end of the intellectual spectrum, neither did we have a dictionary or an encyclopedia.

The teacher's desk had three drawers along the right side with another drawer in the center. A backboard on the desk provided for her modesty.

This little island was our teacher's domain.

Behind the stage and above the middle blackboard was a metal map case affixed to the wall. Four full-color maps printed on canvas cloth could be pulled down for instruction and retracted when not in use, to avoid obscuring the blackboard. The maps were spring-loaded for this convenience. A wooden support dowel ran across the bottom of each map. These Rand McNally maps included one of the United States (all 48 of them); of North and South America; a map of Europe and another of the then-known world. Had Australia been discovered by 1930?

An unknown authority decided to sacrifice practicality for aesthetics by situating the Mill Creek School building so that its (only) door faced Calla Road to the north. This substantial door and the two windows occupied most of the north wall-- leaving no room for maps. (Patmos and Boswell Schools faced south, thus were exempt from this geographical misfortune. Goshen Center suffered the same fate as Mill Creek.)

To wit: our building got fouled up by the lay of the land. The architect had more on his mind than Rand McNally & Company maps, which should have been hung on the north wall. Of course the School Board wanted the entrance to face traffic, but the parcel was on the south side of the road. This vanity (of sorts) dictated our maps could not be hung on the north wall.

And there was the rub.

Map placement on an east, south or west wall would confuse the likes of Magellan. As a first grader myself, contemplating our maps hanging from the south wall, I concluded: "east is west and west is east." I got thoroughly turned around. I know a certain crack navigator (sitting to my west side) [my co-author] who to this day, confesses she must physically face north before being able to read a map or (while driving) flips the map around so that north on the street map aligns with geographical north.

Let's say a certain Miss Lottie Loblolly trotted down the school steps and turned right in order to travel east up Calla Road. Eventually, she'd wind up in California, according to the orientation of our school map. Or, if she turned... (boy, I'm still confused! I'm as turned around today as I was back then) ...if Lottie turned left to travel west toward Bob Boyd's shack and kept on going, she would end up in New York City. I hope readers can comprehend this because—

Picture it! If facing a map on a south wall you'd perceive New York, with the Atlantic Ocean beyond, to the west and California and the Pacific Ocean to the east. Thus I became convinced east was west and west was east.

[Neither of the authors recommends trying this experiment at home.]

At age 6, I knew nil about California or New York. I was too young to fathom such distances, so destinations beyond Boyd's Corners were outside my sphere of influence. In sixth grade, however, on family automobile trips, I perused my dad's road maps. I gathered then that our school map was hung backwards-- rather, that the school itself was turned around! Oh, my gosh! After this breach of innocence, I was befuddled for years about true east and true west. It took ages to re-orient my sense of direction so I could picture where one state was in relation to another. Even today, I must visually visualize, by facing north, pointing east with my right hand, such that west falls into place. That architectural decision to orient the school as such created a dizzying conundrum for me for some quite while. Is there a scientific name for this malady?

The west wall in the schoolhouse had four windows, matching the east wall. Nothing hung on this west wall: no blackboards, no maps, no pictures, no sacred or profane paraphernalia to distract a student's wandering eye — further evidence of the Trustees' spartan approach to interior design.

Coming full circle (or, full rectangle): on the portion of the north wall behind the furnace was the tenth and final window in the schoolhouse.

The interior walls of the red brick building were plastered, then painted dull white. The entire room was about 25 foot wide by 50 foot deep. The flooring was tongue-and-groove oak— a solid floor. The floor was devoid of rugs or carpeting, but a burlap sack underneath our galoshes (parked near the door) wicked up rain, mud and snow. We had no janitor, so I don't know who swept the floor. Our teacher likely delegated this dry-as-dust task to the renegade-of-the-day (could've been me on occasion except for the fact that I was a model child). The dropped ceiling was decorated with embossed tin squares— painted white also. I have to speculate about lights on the ceiling, with pull strings to turn them on and off— seems there were no light switches on the walls.

The room was austere. The windows had no curtains, walloping window blinds or other adornments.

The children's desks were in the center of this substantial room. In a one-room school, the teacher was required to cover six individual grade levels and allot her time proportionately among the grades.

How did she do it!

I use the term "she" since the majority of gradeschool-teacher hires were women; further, these bachelorettes were fired immediately upon upgrading (or downgrading) to a matrimonial status. (The dirty birds did this to Flo. She had been determined to get an education. Like her uncles Emerson and Fred before her, achieving a college education was a rare feat among rural, or any, Americans. Her goal in life was to teach school and she accomplished every bit of that. After four years, she was forced to quit teaching when she married-- it was school policy. She was glad to be asked to return about 20 years later by another school district. Apparently some administrator deemed it wasn't so indecent for married women to teach after all.)

The School Board allowed male teachers upon marriage to keep their jobs.

At any given time there were 16 and no more than 18 students in our school—more than enough for our lone teacher to handle. Occasionally an influenza, measles or scarlet fever epidemic diminished our ranks (temporarily). Even Flo succumbed to enough illnesses that she was made to repeat sixth grade.

Our desks were arranged in columns according to grade level: eldest near the frosty, east windows and the first graders along the cozy west wall by the furnace-- lucky little squirts. The heavy cast-iron frame of each desk was screwed securely to the floor-- this consignment no doubt was the ingenious inspiration of some humorless school administrator to minimize squirming. Each desk had a hinged lid to allow storage of a primer, notebooks, papers, pencils, and more essential sartorial *accoutrements* like gum, slingshots and peashooters. The attached seat was hinged. Thus, it lifted up to allow ease of exit. Those wooden seats were hard and uncomfortable. Why my mother warned us against sitting on the cement porch steps at home for a few minutes, without concern about our getting piles from sitting on those hard school seats for years, is beyond me.

The desks were graduated in size to fit students from 6 to 12 years old.

♪ ♫ ♪

My first teacher was Miss Elvira Smith. I wish I could remember what she looked like. She taught me from first grade through third. I imagine Miss Smith to have been at the ripe age of 20 when she took the helm of Mill Creek School. She was probably just out of normal school and likely grabbed the first job that came along. That would explain why she was so far from home. In May 1931 she did me an extraordinary kindness at the end of first grade.

At the end the school year in 1932, Miss Smith permanently left Mill Creek School. She and her sister were both one-room schoolteachers from Granville, Ohio (near Columbus). They both went back home to live. Maybe the sisters were homesick— Goshen Township was 138 miles northeast of Granville. I have no idea how she got to school every day. She could have had a hand-me-down Model-T automobile. Nor do I recall where she lived, but it must have been close by. Miss Smith boarded with a local farm family as there were no apartments and teachers could not afford to buy a house. Unheard of. All one-room school teachers-- women and men alike-- needed to secure room and board with a nearby rural family. Miss Smith was adequately educated, personable, but intolerant of any student trying to take advantage of her good nature. She brooked no nonsense from ornery boys pulling girls' hair, whispering in class, talking loudly, teasing younger kids or generally being disruptive. She stood for none of that. She keenly sifted eager learners from the chaff of kids who were only there because it was required by law. She could distinguish between eager learners versus desk loungers.

Miss Clara Boyer filled Elvira Smith's vacancy. Miss Boyer was stout and wore her chestnut hair in a tight bun. This blue-eyed lady with rosy cheeks had her pupils' interest at heart. I don't know where she was from. She was kind, considerate— had a good sense of humor. At the time, she was probably 22 years old— having graduated from one of Ohio's normal schools that had been founded to educate elementary-school instructors.

A highlight of my schooldays was a circuit music teacher who came by every Thursday afternoon to lead us in song. To this day I cannot remember her name but she was an outgoing lady. Boy that was a highlight, too! It broke up the monotony of the school day, especially in winter. She was so enthusiastic about her music.

---

*M*ISS _____'S JOB WAS TO VISIT EACH OF GOSHEN TOWNSHIP'S FOUR ONE-ROOM SCHOOLHOUSES ONCE A WEEK TO TEACH MUSIC (--WISH I COULD RECALL HER NAME!). IT MAKES ME WONDER WHAT SHE DID ON THE FIFTH DAY. LIKELY SHE STAYED AT HOME TO COMPOSE HERSELF. ♪ ♫♪

---

Although I do not recall her name I do recall she sought to put some joy into our hearts. She taught us to sing "America the Beautiful" and "The Battle Hymn of the Republic" with its fateful lightning and trampling of grapes. The song "God Bless America" existed then but had not been popularized yet— I didn't hear that song until high school. All of us kids' favorite was a whimsical

American nonsensical ditty, "The Walloping Window Blind." These are the verses as I remember them:

*A* CAPITAL SHIP FOR AN OCEAN SHIP
WAS THE WALLOPING WINDOW-BLIND
NO WIND THAT BLEW DISMAYED THE CREW
OR TROUBLED THE CAPTAIN'S MIND
THE MAN AT THE WHEEL WAS MADE TO CONCEAL
THE WILDEST WIND THAT BLEW
AND IT OFTEN APPEARED WHEN THE GALE HAD CLEARED
HE'D BEEN IN HIS BUNK BELOW.

THE BOATSWAIN'S MATE WAS VERY SEDATE...

CHORUS:
SO BLOW YE WINDS HEIGH HO, A SAILING WE WILL GO
WE STAY NO MORE ON ENGLAND'S SHORE
SO LET THE MUSIC PLAY-AY-AY
WE'RE OFF ON THE MORNING TRAIN
AND CROSS THE ROVING MAIN
I'M OFF TO MY LOVE WITH A BOXING GLOVE
TEN THOUSAND MILES AWAY...

--AFTER CHARLES EDWARD CARRYL

I learned to appreciate music from my now-anonymous teacher. She also taught us "My Old Kentucky Home," "Carry Me Back to Old Virginny," "When Johnny Comes Marching Home," "Camptown Races," "Swanee River" and "K-K-K-Katy," as I recall t:

> ...**K**-K-K-KATY, BEAUTIFUL LADY,
> YOU ARE THE ONLY ONE THAT I ADORE;
> WHEN THE MOON SHINES,
> OVER THE COW SHED,
> I'LL BE WAITING AT THE KA-KA-KITCHEN DOOR...
>
> --AFTER GEOFFREY O'HARA

In the morning, we learned Reading, Writing and Arithmetic, which was not called "Math."

At noon our teacher dismissed us for lunch. We stormed the shelf near the coat hooks, which held our lunches. In the mornings before school, Doris and Elaine had prepared our lunches. Mother was busy elsewhere in the kitchen. They started with two slices of Mother's irresistible homemade bread, spread with her sweet butter. Some days they merely sprinkled some white sugar (the filling) on the buttered bread. Other days it was Mother's homemade peach or strawberry preserves.

We only had meat sandwiches if there was ham or bacon left over from breakfast. A leftover fried egg made for a sumptuous meal. Vegetable sandwiches such as tomato, cucumber and onion were unknown among our *côterie* and we didn't grow lettuce. We only had fresh vegetables in late summer when school was out.

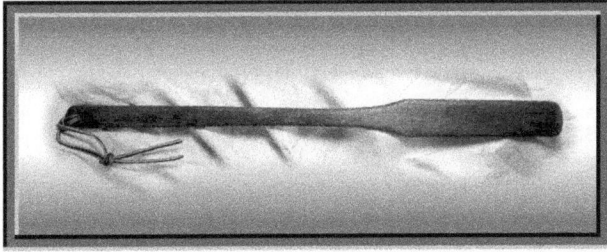

Another version on this theme was the reviled apple-butter sandwich. Apple butter is far more watery than jam or even jelly. Although my sisters smeared the sandwich with dairy butter before laying on the apple butter, the bread labored admirably all morning long like a sponge to absorb most (if not all) the water from the apple butter. By lunchtime my forlorn sandwich had become a soggy mess. It was like having to eat rain-soaked bread puddled in a birdbath.

"...*N*EITHER SNOW NOR SLEET NOR DARK OF NIGHT CAN KEEP THIS BREAD FROM SOAKING UP THE APPLE BUTTER..."

We had no fruit— fresh nor dried—no bananas, no oranges, no peaches (peaches were out in summer... but so was school), no snacks such as cream-filled sponge cake, no cookies. Lunch was only a sandwich wrapped in a page of the Vindy, after Dad had read it, secured with a red rubber band. Thus if a particular day was apple-butter sandwich day, I had little choice but to eat the *sloggy* mess or go hungry.

To this day I cannot bring myself to go near apple butter.

We ate lunch at our desks during inclement weather. If nice out, we were allowed to take our lunches outside, to sit on the front steps or on the grass. The schoolhouse had a pump and sink indoors, next to the furnace. Well water provided the only beverage for washing down a dry sandwich or helping erase the taste of a sodden apple-butter one.

After eating lunch, we played games. Hide and seek, Red Rover, softball and tag were favorites when it was warm enough. Sledding or snowball fighting commenced as the weather permitted.

This narrative circumscribes our teachers, school activities and the interior of the school. Without us, Mill Creek School was just a cold, empty structure. Our teacher and the students made the building come alive.

# VIGNETTE: ELECTION-VICTORY PUNCH

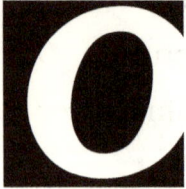

O N MY SOAPBOX I PROCLAIM: "WHEN ELECTED PRESIDENT, ALL SCHOOL MAPS WILL BE PLACED ON NORTH WALLS AND 'AMERICA THE BEAUTIFUL' WILL BE ENACTED AS THE OFFICIAL NATIONAL ANTHEM. FLUTE MUSIC WILL BE OUTLAWED ON PUBLIC RADIO STATIONS."

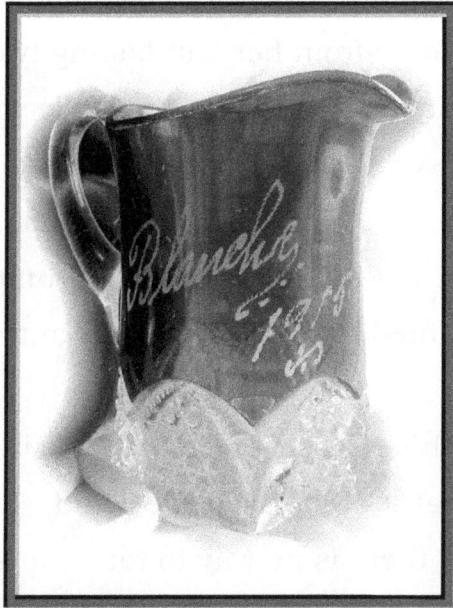

# CHAPTER 10:
## A FORMAL WEEKDAY LUNCHEON.

*"...PUT ON YOUR BIB AND TUCK IN..."*

--MOTHER

URING the week, while the rest of us are at school, Homer is at home with Mother. He is 4.

And still a baby.

Mother prepares a simple lunch. She reheats the coffee from breakfast. The stove is going. She's baking six loaves of her hearty bread. She puts the coffeepot on a burner. She slices a couple pieces of bread from a loaf left over from her last baking two days earlier. She fixes two plates. Each inch-thick slice of bread gets a slather of her sweet-cream butter. She sprinkles white sugar on top. The coffee, hot but not boiling, gets sweetened with milk. Mother pours an ample amount of the caramel-colored, strong, hot liquid onto the buttered, sugared bread.

We call this "coffee bread." To us it is a delicacy. Homer would eat it every day if he could. It is really good (I loved it). But there is no way to tote it to school. (Why I love soggy coffee bread but not soggy apple-butter bread is puzzling.) Mother helps Homer cut up the bread. His appetite is satisfied with just one slice. (Can you imagine a simple fare that brought such enjoyment to us?)

Mother finishes her coffee bread and a cup of coffee. She clears the table and sets the dishes in the sink. She will allow herself the indulgence of leaving the dishes until later, just this time. Homer lies down on the couch in the living room. Mother covers him with one of her patchwork quilts. He drops off to sleep. Mother drags her wicker rocking chair over to the floor register. She positions it so her legs will catch some of the heat coming up from the furnace.

This is her license: a half hour respite.

Mother sits and sighs. It is her time to read the new Farm & Dairy or a Good Housekeeping that one of the ladies had given her at Lodge. Mother is always on the lookout for new recipes. She likes to introduce us to new dishes. And it is a way of avoiding monotony in her life.

Mother's head drops to her chest and she dozes off for a...

# VIGNETTE: BATHTUB PUNCH.

**h**AD FRANCES WILLARD, THE GREAT TEMPERANCE-MOVEMENT LEADER, WHOSE PHOTO DILIGENTLY WATCHED OVER US IN THE ONE-ROOM SCHOOLHOUSE, KNOWN OUR DAD WAS MAKING PROHIBITION BEER IN THE BATHTUB AT HOME-- HER PICTURE WOULD'VE FLOWN OFF THE WALL.

--c. 1933

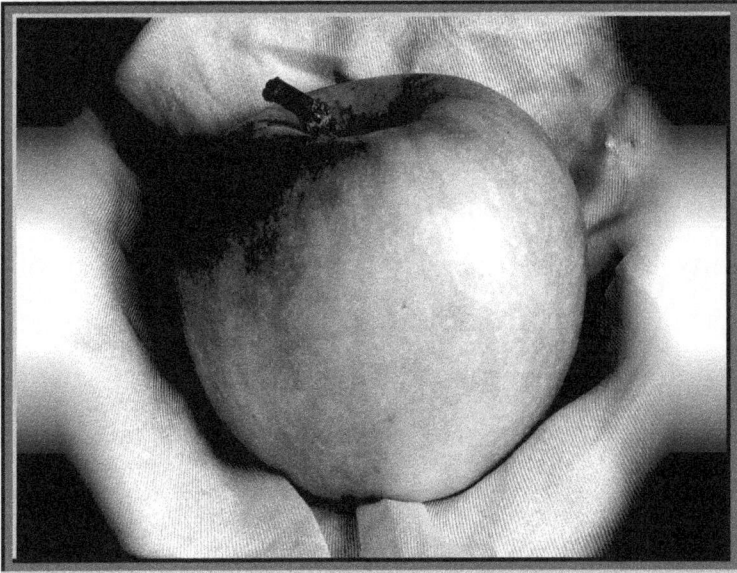

# CHAPTER 11:
## THE STUDENTS.

*"...AN APPLE FOR THE TEASER..."*

**b**ULLIES and their antics comprise my most enduring memories from the five years I spent in our one-room schoolhouse (consider the impress- sion Bobby Boyd left on me). It wasn't all bad though— I wasn't the only one he bullied at Mill Creek.

A shy student certainly, I was eager to learn. The other students impressed me, in so much as there were so many of them and they seemed so much older. I comported myself studiously right into the dubious honor of becoming teacher's pet. I paid attention to Miss Smith and what she expected of and from us: to behave and to avoid emulating rapscallions like Steve Sherlock and his *rumpus interrupticusses.*

But my status as teacher's favorite was not to exempt me from reprimand.

In first grade I was left-handed. Come to think of it I still am. Three of us six Woolf kids were left-handers: Martha Elaine, Flo and I. Thinking it kind of neat, I boasted about it. One day, Elvira Smith deemed my sister should become a right-hander and set out to convert Elaine, who endured this *argumentum baculinum* for months.

"I told you!" Miss Smith said, swinging around the aisle. She brandished a wooden ruler and repeatedly rapped Elaine's knuckles hard. "You will right with your write hand!"Flustered! "I mean, write with the right hand!"

This trial was in vain. Elaine remains, about 80 years later, a southpaw. What business was it of a teacher, at what emotional cost and to what end! I can't imagine why Miss Smith had such strong feelings about it because she didn't pick on me, a lefty too. Why wasn't I singled out for this torment? Elaine no more succumbed to this coercion than our family did to Fr. Coughlin's rantings.

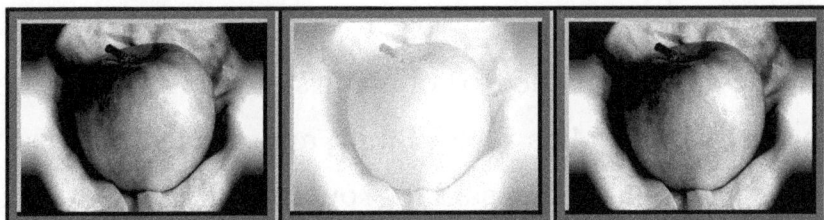

By the age of 6, my blonde hair had turned darker, still with straight bangs bearing proof of Flo's bowl haircuts. In first grade, I was a scrawny kid of average height, so I looked to Elaine and Doris to protect me from bullies. Yet, attending school was a happy time for me, like being inducted into Our Gang or included in a club.

Typically we wore homemade cotton dresses and white cotton ankle socks and infamous underwear. The socks always drooped. Our shoes were clumpy Oxfords with heavy leather soles. Nothing fancy or classy, always re-soled by my dad at his shoe last— not the last time but it made a lasting impression. (By seventh grade, we were required to have tennis shoes for gymnasium class. Before that, I never even saw a pair of gym shoes.)

Also in first grade with me were Leota Ellen (Bobbie Boyd's younger sister) and Helen Myers. Leota had long, curly blonde hair, full cheeks and blue eyes. She was heavy-set. She truly was a nice-looking girl compared to me. I was skinny. She was really a pleasant little girl. This trio comprised the entire first grade: Leota, Helen and I.

One day, at the end of my first year in school, in the spring of 1931, Miss Elvira Smith approached my desk.

"Marcella," she said. "You will NOT be attending second grade in the fall with Helen and Leota Ellen ..."

My heart dropped! My sister Flo had been made to repeat sixth grade. Was the same indignity visiting upon me? And, for what infraction?

"...Wha-aay--..." I started to ask.

"...I have <u>advanced</u> you," she continued. I could hardly believe my ears or my good fortune. She told me to report to the third grade in the fall.

This entailed skipping an entire aisle.

This was the extraordinary gesture Elvira Smith bestowed upon me. By singling me out, recognizing me above all the others, she announced to the world that I was smarter than the average bear. So far as I know, I was the only student who bypassed a grade at Mill Creek.

That particular day in May 1931, I didn't lag behind Doris and Elaine on the walk home. I skipped ahead to be the first to break the news about being skipped ahead.

"Mother!" I said, crashing in through the screen door. Let it slam! I was on a mission.

"Don't sla-am the *scree...*!" she said, as I tumbled into the kitchen. "Mother, you won't believe it! Miss Smith skipped me a grade!"

"Slow down," Mother said, "And tell me from the beginning." We went over to the kitchen table and sat down. I told her about my *exceptionary* honor.

"Marcell!" Mother said, "I'm proud of you. I know you are a very smart little girl." I beamed and preened like a peacock and was generally obnoxious to my siblings for the remainder of the evening.

Mother and Dad let me strut.

In the fall of 1931, I thus skipped second grade and jumped right into third. This promotion rendered me a year younger than my classmates through high school. I was aware of this age difference but adjusted adroitly. I felt special. Being deemed smart enough to catch up to the third graders bolstered the confidence I needed to keep up with students a year older.

## SECOND GRADE: ¡SKIPPED!

In September 1931, the third-grade class inherited me through no fault of their own. Helen and Leota Ellen were left behind in second grade, abandoned. These two little girls alone formed the entire second-grade class. The edge was dulled for them by the irony that their single desk was next to mine across the aisle (when kids were petite enough, they sat two to a desk).

My new classmates were another pair of girls. Dorothy VonKaenel (pronounced "VON'-kennel") and Voneta Stanley were both age 8 at the beginning of third grade. I was 7. A big-boned girl with short brown hair, Dorothy was taller than us. Voneta had brown hair, blue eyes and a pleasant temperament.

Across Calla Road from the schoolhouse was the Thomas farm, a 200-acre dairy operation. Their neighbor to the east was the VonKaenel farm, equally full scale. These two farms occupied that entire stretch of Calla Road between 534 to the west and Seacrist Road to the east. Dorothy's mother (whose name I never knew) and her father, Alf VonKaenel, were born in Switzerland. Dorothy's younger siblings were June and Richard. The VonKaenels were partial to Holstein cattle, a breed developed in the Netherlands (not in Holstein, Germany, as popularly assumed). Alf VonKaenel cured only one variety of cheese: <u>Swiss</u> (what a surprise!). Just as our family sold eggs to a cooperative, the VonKaenels wholesaled their milk to a local (dairy) co-op.

Whenever Homer and I visited Dorothy's house, her parents jibber-jabbered away in Swiss in front of us. Quite intimidating—as a kid, I was convinced they were talking about <u>us</u>. Of course, they may have been discussing family business in general or deliberating about things in specific, like switching their herd to a more superior breed such as Jersey, which do happen to give richer milk. (After all, I ought to know— my family's cow was a Jersey.)

The Stanleys lived down Seacrist Road up a long lane to the east. (Hopefully, the reader has gathered that "down" means "south.") I have no knowledge of the Stanley's farm. I never visited their house. Voneta Stanley had an older sister, Vera, who was attending Goshen High School when we were in third grade. (Was Voneta related to the Mr. Stanley who built our house?)

Our cozy little trio stayed together eight years until I transferred to another high school for my junior year.

When I skipped into third grade without passing **GO**, Elaine advanced into fourth grade along with her *compadres*: Bobby Boyd, Margaret Burton, Dale Weingart and Albert Gfeller (pronounced juh-FEL'-ler). Whereas before, I was two grades behind my next-in-line sister, now I was tagging along one grade in arrears of Elaine.

In the same school year (1931 through 1932) the fifth grade compliment was Rosaleen Keeler, and future lip- and me-smackers Willard Thomas and Lois Ann Burton (Margaret's older sister). Rosaleen was a comely lass with a peaches-and-cream complexion. She was a beautiful girl of Irish heritage. The Keelers lived south on Route 534, one mile from Mill Creek and a mile and a half from Boswell School.  There was also Zella Weingart (Dale's older sister) but I have no recollection of her at Mill Creek School. (Elaine says that Zella attended Christytown School.)

In the sixth grade were Roland Cronick (the Cronicks' heritage was Scots) and Steve Sherlock. Farewell to my sister Dodie, Richard Keeler (Rosaleen's older brother) and Ernest Gfeller (Albert's older brother), who had all moved on to Goshen High School, now that they were in seventh grade and I was in third.

Steve Sherlock was an imposing boy, both in age and appearance.  He was too menacing to stand next to. But if I had—well, envision a skimpy David up against Goliath. Steve was stocky with a freckled face.  His bristly, bright red hair stuck up all over his head, as if to announce his nasty disposition in advance.  His red-headed-stepchild appearance was like a movie *cliché*. Steve Sherlock was so different from everyone else.  He resented and scowled his way through school. Steve was an orphan, all odds stacked against him.

A misbehaver, he was angry and sullen and probably justified in all of it and more.

Steve Sherlock had come from the Fairmount Children's Home in Alliance, over in next-door Stark County. This "Oliver Twist with a twist" tale focused on the darker bits. The Fairmount Home was famous (infamous, actually). The Fairmount farmed out these misfortunates for domestic use (and abuse) — even we school kids were privy to the scandal. This subterfuge exempted the Children's Home from feeding, clothing or sheltering those orphans and bolstered a lucky farm family with a free, extra pair of hands. We are not talking about an official adoption process. The orphans— this sorry lot— were taken advantage of by the same institution mandated by the State to protect them. In Steve's case, had his parents died or abandoned him? Which family took him in during our Mill Creek School days? We felt sorry for Steve Sherlock, scapegoat.

Who could blame him.

When Steve misbehaved (often and ongoing: talked out of turn, talked back to the teacher or otherwise disrupted), Miss Boyer notified the Principal of Goshen High School by phone or by mail. Principal Carl Long was a man of average height (about 5 foot 8), of average build with graying black hair. He had a full black mustache and wore rimless glasses along the popular trend.

Prompted by this summons, Mr. Long dropped by for a surprise visit to take Steve in hand. Mr. Long and our teacher conferred privately. Mr. Long wasted no time. He ordered Steve to report to a chair near the furnace, to drop his trousers, lean over the back of the chair where Mr. Long proceeded to beat him with a wooden paddle. Corporal punishment was common. Some devoted father had carved and shaped the paddle out of wood and presented it to Mr. Long. Steve never cried during these public humiliations. This thrashing occurred behind our backs and not one of us dared turn around for a peek. It was embarrassing for all parties concerned— Steve, our teacher and us-- but it must have demeaned Mr. Long, who was at heart a genial, gentle person. As Principal, he was expected to be stern, but he remained fair, too. Steve took his punishment stoically.

Later, no one dared tease Steve about getting a licking or about anything for that matter— he promptly would have beat them up!

Then there was Bobby Boyd, a malefactor in every sense of the word. In the same misfit league as Steve Sherlock, Bobby was younger and not an orphan, so he lacked a good excuse for bad behavior.

Bobby was the only son of that despicable man, Bob Boyd, of the eponymous Boyd's Corner catercorner from Mill Creek School. A daredevil, Bobby relied on his father to extract him from every scrape. Bobby never came to school the next day to announce his father had licked him for acting up in school. In fact, Bob Boyd Sr. seemed to cheer on his son's malfeasance. My dad had no dealings with Mr. Bob Boyd, period. My opinion of the man (independent of my dad's justified contempt) formed later. Living with the Boyds would have transformed a Pollyanna into a miscreant. How Leota Ellen (Bobby's younger sister) survived her childhood in that *dysfamilial functionary* must be left to conjecture.

Of average height, Bobby Boyd had poker-straight hair that hung in his eyes. He nervously brushed his light-brown hair aside, as if signaling he had spotted the next victim of his pranks. Usually a scowl graced his face— certainly not a smile. How do you describe someone who's always plotting something? It was not a scowl (he wasn't angry). It was a smirk. That's it. He was always plotting and smirking.

I do not know if there was a "Mrs. Bob Boyd." I never met Bobby's mother. Let's just assume he might have had one.

Bobby Boyd had riled Miss Smith and, in turn, Miss Boyer, by misbehaving, overall teasing and by his absolute dis-intending to learn.

As a player, he was always in motion.

"You're ugly!" Bobby told Dorothy VonKaenel once. He delighted in tripping younger kids, snapping their bare arms with a rubber band. Like the *bona fide* bully he was, Bobby never dared pick on older boys.

## FOURTH GRADE: 1932-1933.

One spring day in 1933, I incurred Bobby Boyd's wrath and had to pay.

My veneer as teacher's pet had worn thin by then and couldn't save me from a trampling with the grapes of wrath.

The incident started with The Little Rascals, the darlings of Hollywood. They were regulars in the movies (although I never attended a motion-picture cinema until 1937). But everybody else was talking about "Our Gang." Alfalfa, Buckwheat, Darla and Spanky were Our Gang's prime perpetrators. I do not recall all of the remaining club members. I do know the little "pickaninny," Buckwheat, was prominent in that he stood out among the "white" kids. Hollywood inherited the use of pickaninnies as a humor device from vaudeville and from literature before that. [Today, the term offends, but in the 1920's and 30's "pickaninny" was in the American lexicon and still is— I heard it on National Public Radio this morning.]

The Little Rascals were depicted on the cover of my prized possession, a school notebook. Mother had bought it for me at Woolworths 5 & 10 in Salem. At the time of this bloody do, I was in fourth grade and Bobby in fifth—making him <u>two</u> years my senior. (I had to do the math here. Even though he was two years older, he was just one grade ahead of me, courtesy of Miss Smith. Despite her high opinion of my intellect by skipping me into third grade, the math is confounding to this day.) Thinking I was being clever, I penciled in the names of select classmates beside the photographs of the Our Gang members' faces on my notebook. Alfalfa became "WILLARD" Thomas-- both wore eyeglasses. Darla was easily labeled "MARGARET" Burton. Spanky—who knows? But the little pickaninny, Buckwheat, was re-crowned, "BOBBY."

How Bobby Boyd espied his name on my notebook— I don't know. Although... everybody was seated in proximity to each other in the confined space of Mill Creek School. Bobby could have been spying on me as I was deep in concentration, defiling Our Gang. (I can just see myself hunched over the desk, trying to hide my handiwork.) Or, someone tattled on me. But Bobby did see it. And took offense. He scurried up and whinged about it to Miss Boyer. She wasted no time and approached my desk to take a look-see for herself.

There she spotted Buckwheat with his new pet name: BOBBY, clear as the water that gurgled in the crick.

"What is the meaning of this, Marcella?" she asked.

"I dunn-no-o."

"That's all you have to say for yourself?"

"...'ont kno-ow," I said, hanging my head. Miss Boyer had me over a barrel. I was too *discomposed* to mutter anything much more intelligible. Miss Boyer probably thought it was as funny as I did. No doubt she had to choke back a chuckle! But to save face she marched back to her desk. She returned to the scene of the crime, armed and dangerous ("crime" according to Mr. Boyd Jr.).

"Hold out cher hands," she barked. By this time, about 16 other pairs of eyeballs, faces agog, were riveted on this melodrama as it unfolded. Miss Boyer whacked me over the knuckles with her wooden ruler.

"You should know better," she said, before turning away to put up her ruler. "That will teach you not to make fun of people." A few snickers rippled through the heavy air, but no one dared breathe a word lest they invite their own *conflusion* with the ruler.

Meanwhile, I furiously scratched out Bobby's name with a pencil. Bobby was wearing a broad smirk atop his usual smirk, convinced he had won that round. He erred. "BOBBY" was still visible underneath the cross-out next to Buckwheat's head into posterity.

It was commonplace for teachers to smite a student. I was chagrined even though getting whacked didn't hurt that much. Inwardly, my pride stung more than my knuckles stung outwardly. Inwardly, I felt superior because I had pulled a fast one on Bobby Boyd. And I'd like to think some of those other students' snickers were from collusion, not derision. Hah!

Fortunately, this come-off came off in spring. The end of the school year hastened. I had three pesterer-free months to anticipate with the inception of summer.

Thus ended any friendship I may have cultivated with one Bobby Boyd-the-Younger. Miss Boyer forgave me my trespasses. She was an exceptionally kind lady and only punished me because she felt she had to. Miss Boyer was well aware of Bobby Boyd's well-plotted capers.

Had I been as smart as Miss Smith had proclaimed, I would have snuck a leaky, overly-rotten apple into that teaser's (Bobby's) desk when no one was looking— wouldda served him right.

Another character was the school swag-gart— full of himself, confident-- we were too scared of Dale Weingart to call him "Dale Brag-gart." But that's what he was. He called the shots. In Bobby's and Elaine's class, he was two years older than me (again, one grade ahead). He was a sly, savvy gang leader. Dale was tall for his age, slim— dark wavy hair— actually he was quite handsome. He kept his hair combed neatly. He was always well vigilant of his looks. Dale was not a bully type, such as being cruel to animals or mean to little kids. A big tease, he liked to needle everybody yet wanted to stay on the teacher's good side. He knew enough to do just that, maintain that balance. The teacher assigned Dale chores he gladly executed to please her (obligingly so) just to keep in her good graces-- pumping a bucket of water for the kids to drink, using a metal dipper, erasing the blackboard, clapping the erasers, bringing in coal or firing the furnace.

But he loved to tease people— he even came to our house to tease my dad! Of course Dad was on to him.

Dale heckled the younger girls-- including me-- into pulling up our own dresses to expose our undergarments. He got a big kick out of sneaking up behind an Innocent to lift up her dress.

Dale Weingart pulled this stunt on me one day while we were all waiting for the school bus. So it must have happened when I was in fourth or fifth grade because the busses started running in the fall of 1932.

Dale tiptoed behind me. He snappily yanked up the back of my dress and was holding it up by the hem. My *underlings* were seeing sunlight for the first time that day.

"Ha! Oo-Hah! Hawr-rr!" he said, crowing to the other boys. "Her bloomers are made outta SUGAR sacks!"

He made me feel like the laughingstock of the school. It was mortifying to have my *privacies* exposed to the known world.

Actually, those sugar sacks had many uses. Am I digressing? As stated, our sugar was purchased in cloth 50-pound bags—kept in the upstairs landing accessible to the kitchen. We used the white sugar in baking and canning, and sprinkled it on sandwiches, coffee bread and breakfast cereal. Because we were poor, Mother had to take advantage of every scrap of useable cloth she could get her hands on. These sacks she re-used for sewing projects. She made our bloomers, baggy drawers that served as underpants, with elastic at waist and knees. Mother also used sugar-sack material for dish towels, handkerchiefs, pillowcases and slips for our dresses. A sugar sack always hung in the bathroom as a hand towel. (Mother would have made a coverlet for the barn out of them had she had a sufficient number of sugar sacks, you betcha.)

Remarkably— it was rather laughable for Dale to make fun of _me_ when his own family was on Relief— his father Sam Weingart just stayed home and never sought out work-- content to wait on the dole.

Another little girl, pitiably shy, fell victim to Dale's tormenting. After school one spring day, Dale, Bobby and another pally posted themselves in the front yard of the schoolhouse near Calla Road. They found their mark. Helen Myers was 8 years old and in third grade. Even before Dale called out to her, Helen started walking away at a fast clip to avoid the brutes.

"Pull up your dress!" he said, commanding Helen to snap-to. The trio caught up to her. "Show us your bloomers!" the boys chimed. Dale had to work at this— he was intimidating Helen by commanding (and alternately begging) her to lift up her own dress.

The Myers family was a neighbor of the Sam Weingart family. Both families lived west of Route 534 on Western Reserve Road, on the south side. The Myers house was up a long, dirt lane. The Weingart's ramshackle dwelling, long and narrow like a railroad boxcar, was virtually on the road. I imagine Helen's parents were strict, hence her timorous demeanor. She was probably browbeaten at home-- painfully timid.

"Come on, _come on!_" Dale said, goading her. Helen knew if she didn't comply, one of the boys himself would pull up her dress for her. Quite a quandary. She was intimidated and started to cry. She didn't pull her dress all the way up to her chin. Just far enough for them to see the legs of her bloomers-- a token pull, as the hem of her bloomers fell at the knees.

I was standing there about four or five feet away from Helen, off to the side. Witnessing this ordeal, I wished my comic-book hero, Hopalong Cassidy, would have hopped along into the fray to pommel these renegades. I felt humiliated for her, yet stupefied into inaction.

This incident haunted my memories for many years. I never knew if little Helen Myers got home, told her parents and they spanked her; if she didn't tell them and it was on <u>her</u> conscience; or, if someone tattled on her. All speculation but it preyed on my mind.

I wish I could go back and do it over, to vindicate poor little Helen. I'd step into the *frumpus* and kick that *tormentrator* Dale in the shins. I had good clompy shoes to do it with, too. Gee, I still feel bad for Helen.

SEVERAL YEARS LATER, I EVENED THE SCORE. WHEN DALE WAS VISITING ONE DAY, HOMER AND I BORROWED A FEW CONDOMS DALE HID IN HIS CAR. WE TWO KIDS RACED UP TO THE CORNER AT WESTERN RESERVE ROAD. WE BLEW THEM UP LIKE BALLOONS AND TIED A KNOT IN THE END AND POKED AT THEM WITH STICKS.

Another classmate was Willard Thomas. He was no relation to the Miss Willard of temperance fame and of the east schoolhouse wall. Three years my elder, he was in sixth grade when I was in fourth, due to my grade-skipping. Slim, confident and intelligent, he wore glasses. He wasn't blonde but had light brown hair. Willard might have gone on to become a lawyer or into some profession less miasmatical. Willard probably earned at least a master's degree. *Au contraire*, other kids left school at age 15 because they were bored.

Willard's parents owned a thriving, well-kempt farm on the other side of Calla Road, just a half mile east of Mill Creek School. Lois Ann Burton lived directly across the road from the Thomas farm. Willard walked to school together with Lois Anne and her sister, Margaret. Lois Ann was an attractive strawberry blonde. Her hair was long enough to wear in a bun. And she was tall. Trim—cordial— she was a nice girl. She wore glasses too.

One day I made a fowl personal foul. I made the mistake of teasing Willard and Lois Anne during recess. I was *morbally* obligated to do it. After all, I spotted them holding hands in the schoolyard.

"Willard loves Lois Anne!"— I said, yelling, inferring they were boyfriend and girlfriend. It was my turn to be the teaser. Boy did <u>that</u> cause a backlash. They did not appreciate my *inferentials*. Nor did they take it lightly. They both rushed over to me and set about slapping me on my shoulders and head and arms, their arms flapping like chicken wings. They didn't draw blood but they let me know they didn't welcome my being a smart aleck where their affections were concerned. It was just a gradeschool romance. They didn't get married to each other later— but if there were no truth in it at all...then why bother beating me up? And what were they doing holding hands! In the sixth grade!

That was spring of 1933 and I was just finishing fourth grade. My birthday is in July so I was still 8 years old when they whomped me. This was Lois Anne's and Willard's last year at Mill Creek. In the fall, they headed off to Goshen High. So I didn't see those two lovebirds for another two and a half years.

A little time, perhaps, for both of them to cool off.

## FIFTH GRADE: 1933-1934.

In the fall of 1933, I was 9 years old and entered fifth grade. My sister Dodie was in the ninth grade. Goshen High offered two foreign languages: Latin and French. Dodie opted French as her foreign-language credit, taught by Miss Adrian Spahn. One class assignment was to learn by heart the French national anthem in one week. Dodie brought this project home. Miss Spahn expected her students not only to learn the lyrics but also to sing the song out loud in public. Dodie took this homework literally as she sang it out loud and loudly.

When I first heard the song, I vainly assumed the title was eponymous to me. Or, at the least— if "La Marcell-aze" had not been named after me, then I might have been named for it. I had two things going for me: 1) a birth date on Bastille Day (July 14th, France's equivalent of the Fourth of July) and 2) a name coincident with France's national anthem.

After school and into the evening *à la nauséement*, Dodie strolled through the house like the toreador in "Carmen," practicing. A week of listening to her rendition of "La Marseillaise" wore out, but to my avail-- I learned the words *by right rote* along with her. Of course, foreign languages were not taught at my little one-horse school. Learning so much French by proxy gave me a leg up on some of my foolish schoolmates, *cettes Bouchélleurs*. The following represents the words to "La Marseillaise" as I remember them, as *alliterated* by my co-author:

---

...ALONS ENFANT LA PATRIA, LE JOUR DE GUERRE EN NOUS TE REVEILLE. ENTRE NOUS... ENTENDE VOUS DANS LE CAMPANIE... MARCHAND, MARCHAND...

(actual lyrics:) ...ALLONS ENFANTS DE LA PATRIE, LE JOUR DE GLORIE EST ARRIVE! CONTRE NOUS... ENTENDEZ-VOUS DANS LES CAMPAGNES... MARCHONS, MARCHONS...

---

Not bad, eh? I can remember the tune but not all the words. I don't know if any other family members memorized this song along with Dodie and *moi* but they were exposed to it, it was so ramparts—I mean, <u>rampant</u>. Other French tidbits I learned from Doris were:

- ¿Comment t'allez vous?
- Bon jour, Madame et Monsieur
- Adieu!
- Beaucoups
- écolé
- Le Boulevard de... broken dreams
- Passe-moi de pommes de terre... (*sic*)

That is my fifth-grade experience.

## SIXTH GRADE: 1934-1935.

In the fall of 1934, Dorothy VonKaenel, Voneta Stanley and I rode into sixth grade on our high horses. I entered my fifth (and final) year at the darling little Mill Creek School. We were now the top dogs. We had earned the dubious privilege of sitting in the aisle closest to the east (and coldest) wall.

The older students had pushed on ahead of us into Goshen High School, domain of Mr. Carl Long, *PaddleMeister*. Goshen stood near the intersection of Routes 534 and 62 in Damascus, four miles south of our one-room schoolhouse. My sisters Doris and Elaine had advanced and my little brother, Homer, was in third grade at Mill Creek. The students who left us behind there included the Gfellers, the Keelers, the Burtons *and Les Trois Pestilenceurs*: Steve, Bobby and Dale; Golden-Gloves Willard Thomas; and Roland Cronick.

Come to think of it— I can't even picture Bobby Boyd at Goshen. They might've run someone like him outta there on a rail.

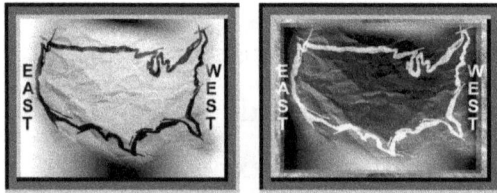

With *Les Enfants Terribles* gone, the air at Mill Creek was decidedly different. Voneta, Dorothy and I became Teacher's Pests—I mean, Pets. Miss Boyer respected us as young ladies. Even she seemed to breathe a sigh of relief to have all the other Pests eradicated. We felt free to hunker down into our studies. Miss Boyer parlayed by assigning us greater responsibilities, such as keeping the blackboards and erasers clean. Our trio was all-girls, so we joined in chores usually reserved for boys: hauling in buckets of coal, stoking the furnace, sweeping the floor, picking up wastepaper. We mothered the first and second graders, helped the younger kids with their boots.

Homer was in third grade with June VonKaenel, Dorothy's little sister. Bobby Phyllis lived on Seacrist Road with his family— he was in second grade. Dorothy's little brother, Richard VonKaenel, was in first grade.

Students who attended Mill Creek in later years included Jesse and Roger Martig and their little sister; Donnie and Marcia Stratton; and Bobby Biery.

As sixth graders then, Dorothy, Voneta and I became the Queen Bees of Mill Creek. During recess, we became the final arbiters in playground disputes. We relished now having the prerogative of choosing our <u>own</u> sides for the various games or team sports we played. This ended the sting of that nefarious practice: my getting called on <u>last</u> (or not at all) for playground games.

SCHOOL RECITATION: **WHY ARE FIRE ENGINES RED?** BECAUSE BOOKS ARE READ, TOO, AND 2 AND 2 ARE 4, AND 4 TIMES 3 MAKES 12, AND 12 INCHES MAKE A RULER, AND A RULER IS QUEEN MARY, AND THE QUEEN MARY IS A SHIP, AND SHIPS SAIL THE OCEAN, AND THE OCEAN HAS FISH, AND THE FISH HAVE FINS, AND THE FINNS FOUGHT THE RUSSIANS, AND THE RUSSIANS ARE RED, AND THAT'S WHY FIRE ENGINES ARE RED-- BECAUSE THEY'RE ALWAYS RUSHIN'.

# VIGNETTE: THE RUNNING BOARD.

WEST ON WESTERN RESERVE ROAD WERE SEVERAL DWELLINGS, SHABBILY-BUILT HOUSES. ON THE RIGHT SIDE HEADING WEST, ABOUT A HALF MILE DOWN AND ACROSS THE LITTLE CRICK, LIVED CHARLEY DUDLEY OF BREEDING-BOAR FAME. AN UNKEMPT MAN, THIS HARD-SCRABBLE FARMER CARED NOT A WHIT ABOUT HIS APPEARANCE. HE WORE DIRTY OVERALLS SPRITZED WITH TOBACCO STAINS, DIDN'T SHAVE ON A REGULAR BASIS AND LIKED HIS LIQUOR. MY DAD SHAVED EVERY MORNING AND USUALLY LOOKED NEAT WITH HIS DENIM SHIRT AND OVERALLS FASTENED WITH A LEATHER BELT. THIS BELT WAS HANDY FOR PULLING OUT OF ITS LOOPS TO GIVE US KIDS A LICKING WHEN WE HAD MISCONSTRUED THE RULES. ONE RULE WAS NEVER TO JUMP ONTO A RUNNING BOARD OF A CAR, WHETHER STATIONARY OR MOVING. JUMPING ONTO CARS WAS GREAT SPORT AND ALMOST EXPECTED OF HOMER AND ME. AS VISITORS DROVE INTO THE DRIVEWAY, WE RAN UP BEHIND, HOPPED ON BOARD THE STILL-MOVING CAR AND POKED OUR HEADS IN THE WINDOW TO GREET THE OCCUPANTS. THIS MUST HAVE STUNNED THE DRIVER. WE WERE JUST BEING FRIENDLY. DAD TOLD US MANY TIMES TO REFRAIN FROM THIS DANGEROUS PRACTICE BUT WE DID IT ANYWAY. ONE TIME, WHEN SOME VISITORS HAD LEFT, DAD WASTED NO TIME IN PULLING OFF HIS BELT TO GIVE US A GOOD WHACKING ON OUR BEHINDS. SOMETIMES, IF WE HAD DISOBEYED HIS RULES, HE SWITCHED US WITH A PRIVET-HEDGE BRANCH. OUTRAGED, WE SCURRIED CRYING TO MOTHER WHO WANTED TO CONSOLE US, BUT WE KNEW ENOUGH NOT TO CROSS FATHER AND SHE KNEW ENOUGH NOT TO TAKE OUR SIDE AGAINST HIM. HOMER AND I, STILL SOBBING, LAY DOWN ON THE DAVENPORT AND CRIED OURSELVES TO SLEEP.

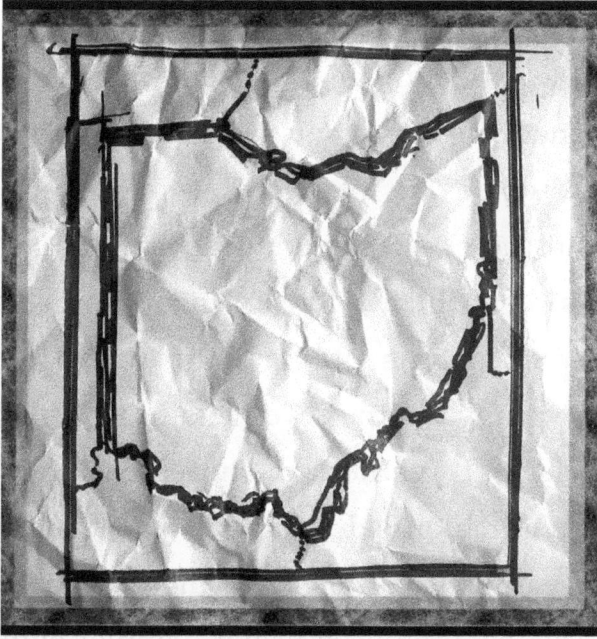

# CHAPTER 12:
## GAMES WE PLAYED AT SCHOOL.

**"*YOU'RE 'IT,' YA DUM BUNNY.*"**

RECESS began at noon. We students didn't have wristwatches but our teacher had one. She let us know when it was noon, time for lunch.

Our lunch was our lunch. It consisted of a sandwich and maybe a slug of water to wash it down, period. We had neither snacks to pack into lunches nor to eat between meals.  The Twinkie was invented in 1930. Yet my dad was too practical to spend money on Twinkies (or other snack foods) when we had homemade baked goods after supper.  No ice-cold Cokes.  No ice.

'Round-the-clock snacking as a national pastime, as well as convenient convenience stores fueled by prepackaged foods, was a thing of the future.

During rainy weather, we ate our sandwiches at our desks.  In clement weather, we shoved each other out the door and ate lunch outside, perhaps on the stone step.

After eating, a straggler could join a game, any game in progress, organized or not. Popular games among us youngsters were hide and seek, tag and Red Rover.

Due to the layout of the school grounds, kids didn't have much choice of cover while playing hide and seek. Everyone learned all the hiding places quickly.  For concealment, we jumped into the deep ditch alongside Calla Road, stood behind the privies or behind trees (which didn't hide errant arms & legs), kneeled alongside the coal house adjoining the school or crouched close to the teacher's jalopy.

"Ollie-Ollie-in-free," the seeker yelled, admitting defeat and ending the game of hide and seek. Anyone still hiding was allowed to come in free and won— having outsmarted the seeker. (As a kid, I always wondered who "Ollie" was. Now my co-pilot informs me was *Kiddish* for "All Ye, All Ye, in free.")

For team sports, we had no football or basketball equipment, so we played Red Rover. A line of students faced another, with arms outstretched in a chain, all hands clasped fiercely (except one hand on either end). One player at a time sprinted to the other side while scanning for the weak link. The goal was to break through the line. If unsuccessful, that player had to join the defense line, which then called over another runner.

Anyone who successfully unclasped a set of hands on the line was allowed to return to the offensive side, their home queue-- the offense had won thereby a turn at calling a challenger.

"Red Rover, Red Rover," we sang at the top of our lungs, uniformly off-key, for example: "Let Dorothy come over." We filled in the name of the student who was up next, picked at random. Of course the popular kids got selected to go over first, so it was not exactly random. I was mostly-always selected last about 10 times out of 9 or not at all if 1:00 rolled around too soon—time for afternoon classes.

Tag and Red Rover provided vigorous exercise. Hide and seek was passive, lots of waiting around.

We had no decent balls to play with. We had to make do with what we had. We staged baseball games. Our old excuse of a ball had a hard crust and spongy innards. A little larger than a tennis ball, it had lost its bounce and a few chunks of itself from hard use. Through time, it cracked and pitted. A discarded, weathered wooden slat sufficed for a bat, likely a one-by-four (a two-by-four would have been too ungainly).

The gentle hill behind the school led down to the outhouses. The slope was inadequate for proper spacing of bases, so baseball games were hardly a challenge. The red ball rolled down the hill and a chase ensued. If I were the one in pursuit, sometimes I stopped to use the girls' privy while I was down there. This *ablugation* took place amidst shouts from the ranks of the halted game.

"Hey! C'mon!" players said, shouting from atop the hill. "Bring us the ball, ya dummy!"

"Gotta GO!" I said, yelling through the slats in the privy door. If I really had to go, I didn't bother throwing the ball to them beforehand— it was uphill and I had a scrawny arm. While the kids waited I sang to myself.

"Way down upon the Scrawnee River," I crooned, "far, far from Rome…"

A daunting game was "Anti-Over," an Ohio colloquialism for "Antony-Over." Daunting— at least to the first and second graders. Older students were obligated to let them play because there were less than 18 kids in the whole school. This simple game called for a line to form along the east and west sides of the schoolhouse. The aim was for a player to throw the same fossilized ball to the line of gameskids on the far side.

"Anti-Over!" the kids on the other side chanted. "Anti-Over, c'mon!" Meanwhile, the kids along the throwing line deliberated as to who should be the hurler.

They never chose me.

"Throw it already!" the others said, yelling. "You dumb bunnies!" Neither Miss Smith nor Miss Boyer tolerated name-calling, so at that particular moment the teacher might have been in the privy.

The roof was about 20 foot high, maybe more. The pitched roof was high and steep, extremely tough for a *gawkward* kid like me to throw the ball not only to that height— but also to clear the peak of the roof. But I kept at it. Oft'times, the ball hit the top of the coal bin and *flounced* ("b<u>ounced</u> with <u>fl</u>air") up in the air and rolled down the hill underneath the teacher's Model T. A recalcitrant little kid was sent to scramble under the car to retrieve the recalcitrant ball.

---

... *T*HE ROOF IS HIGH AND DARK AND STEEP AND I HAVE PROMISES TO KEEP... AND MILES TO GO BEFORE I WEEP... (FORGIVE THE *PERJURISM*.)

---

The fun part was when the ball cleanly cleared the peak of the roof. That was the whole point.

It took me an entire summer to perfect Anti-Over by throwing a ball over our house, in-between farm chores. Homer posted himself on the other side of the house. We took turns throwing the ball over. Our roof had gutters so we had to be careful. I got so proficient, I won all the time once school began again. The reprobates had flown. Voneta, Dorothy and I were left to run the show. I even beat some of the remaining boys by then at Anti-Over.

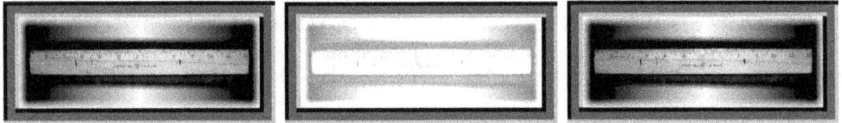

In winter, a breakneck hill across Calla Road on the Thomas farm provided an ideal venue for sled riding—convenient too, as it was in front of our schoolhouse. My family owned a handsome Flexible Flyer sled. Its bright red runners contrasted proudly with a natural wood finish emblazoned with the distinctive eagle trademark. My dad permitted us to tug the Flyer to school during those frigid Ohio winters. We piled on, three at a time, to sled down the hill. At the bottom, our progress was abruptly halted by an iced-over marsh, its reeds sticking up. Pulling the sled back up top was dully repetitive but the anticipation of another daring ride downhill was well worth it.

At the end of May 1935, my one-room-school days ended, sadly enough. Voneta Stanley, Dorothy VonKaenel and I had a brief summer to *metamorphosize* from sixth-grade small fry in the little pond at Mill Creek into big fish in the big pond at Goshen High School. We were called on to evolve our *pamperling* selves into toeing the line— you might say we became "G'Ocean Liners." What a shock, learning to swim in a (Mill) Creek that emptied too soon into a(n) (G)Oshen. We left behind our diminutive schoolhouse with its handful of students to attend a leviathan like Goshen with its student body of two hundred or so. We were called on to grow up fast.

Students younger than us who attended Mill Creek beyond 1935, as discussed, included Jesse and Roger Martig and their little sister; Bobby Biery; Donnie and Marcia Stratton; and, last but not least, little baby Homer.

I do not recall specifically the process of learning to connect the A B C's *per se* with the magic of the spoken and printed word, or to associate "1, 2, 3...10" *per se* with the magic of arithmetic. I do know I was a fast learner. Miss Smith first recognized this trait, God bless her, and letting me skip second grade incited me to excel. In any event, I took advantage by doing my homework and chores quickly to leave time for leisure reading in order to broaden my horizons.

I have spent the rest of my life reading more than my share.

The Martig brothers, aforementioned, in adulthood bought the Mill Creek School building after the one-room facility was closed for all time. The structure was converted on-site into a private residence.

The building still stands today. The belfry is gone and a more-recent addition masks the original west side of the building. The teacher's flivver is gone from the driveway forevermore. The privies are gone. An image from the early 1900's-- of a teacher, her white shirtwaist tucked into an ankle-length dark skirt, standing beside her clutch of a dozen or so students (who are seated on the front lawn) — is a faded photograph or a faded memory...

# IT GOES WITH THE LIFE.

DORIS WAS IN THE BATHROOM AT HOME, MINISTERING TO HER PERSONAL HYGEINE. AT THE TIME, I WAS ABOUT 10. I CAME ALONG AND DID NOT REALIZE THE BATHROOM WAS OCCUPIED. WITHOUT KNOCKING, I OPENED THE DOOR AND SAW DODIE STANDING IN THERE HANDLING A BLOODIED RAG. IT WAS MADE FROM SUGAR-SACK REMNANTS. IT WAS NOT A WHOLE SUGAR SACK, JUST FOLDED-UP RAGS. HERE WAS MY FIRST ENCOUNTER WITH THE NOTION OF MENSTRUATION. NO ONE— MY MOTHER, SISTERS OR SCHOOLKIDS— HAD BROACHED THE SUBJECT TO ME. I HAD BEEN ABANDONED TO ABJECT IGNORANCE. DODIE WAS ABOUT 15. SHE WAS JUST AS STARTLED TO SEE <u>ME</u> AS I WAS TO SEE ALL THAT <u>BLOOD</u>.

"GIT OUTTA HERE!" SHE YELLED AS SHE SWUNG AWAY FROM ME. I BACKED OUT OF THE BATHROOM IN HIGH GEAR. SHE SLAMMED THE DOOR BEHIND ME. MOTHER WAS IN THE LIVING ROOM INNOCENTLY READING THE VINDICATOR.

"MOM, WHY IS DODIE BLEEDING?" I SAID, RUNNING INTO THE ROOM. MOTHER WAS DUMBSTRUCK. I HAD PULLED HER UP SHORT. A LONG PAUSE FOLLOWED. THINGS LIKE THAT WERE SIMPLY NOT DISCUSSED. I STOOD THERE BLINKING BACK TEARS AS MOTHER FORMULATED HER EXPLANATION.

"IT GOES WITH THE LIFE," MOM FINALLY SAID. I WAS MORE PERPLEXED THAN EVER. DURING THE NEXT SEVERAL DAYS, DODIE AND I AVOIDED LOOKING AT EACH OTHER ACROSS THE KITCHEN TABLE BECAUSE WE WERE BOTH SO EMBARASSED.

--C. 1934

# RECIPE: BAKED CUSTARD.

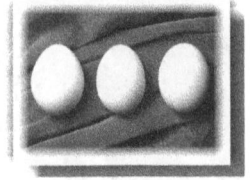

*m* **ARCELLA:** "My mother, Blanche, made custard once a week. Her baked custard and custard pies were my favorite desserts. Custard was easy to make. Of course, with the poultry farm, she had plenty of fresh eggs. My whole family appreciated this treat. Mother's custard was rich yellow, thick and creamy, not watery. I'd like to have a dish of it right now."

JODY: "I wish I had my grandma Blanche's recipe cards. I've had to guess at all her recipes. My mother, Marcella, claims my recipe here is 'getting close' to the desserts she remembers from the 1930's. I toy with the oven temperature and ingredients. Blanche never put raisins in her egg custard. Sometimes I do—delicious."

- 2 DOZEN FARM-FRESH EGGS, FROM FREE-RANGE CHICKENS, FEEDING ON FLAXSEED MEAL AND BUGS
- 2 QTS. MILK, RAW, UNPASTEURIZED, FROM A FARM
- 3 TBSP. ORGANIC ALLSPICE-CINNAMON-NUTMEG SPICES
- ¼ CUP (OR TO-TASTE) ORGANIC, RAW, BLUE AGAVE NECTAR (OR SUGAR)
- 3 TBSP. ORGANIC VANILLA (MORE IF YOU CAN AFFORD IT)

**ALLOW** MILK TO ADJUST TO ROOM TEMPERATURE. Whip eggs 'til frothy. Whip some more. Add milk a little at a time while still whipping eggs. Add spice mix, vanilla (& raisins if desired). Whip a bit more. Desired consistency: frothy.

**BAKE** AT 275 °F. 20 MINUTES. Increase heat to 315 °F. for another 40 min. Total baking time: 1 hour (a knife inserted into custard should come out clean). LET COOL.

# VICTUAL RITUALS.

# CHAPTER 13:
## MY DAD.

*"MY EAST LEG IS ACTING UP."*

**--DAD**

AD'S domain was the garage as much as the kitchen was Mother's. Two buildings stood in proximity to our house. One was the privy. The other, the garage, was handy on several counts. Close to the house, the garage stored our cars and served as Dad's workshop-- just down the back porch steps, across the drive to the south about twenty feet.

The garage was already there when my folks moved to the house in 1917.  Mr. Sumner Stanley, as stated, was a carpenter and a capable one at that.  He had built the house and garage and barn.

The garage was painted white with sage green trim. There were three windows in the garage:  two on the west wall facing Route 534 and one on the south overlooking the privy. The low-peaked roof was covered with asphalt shingles (not slate to match the house), a clue indicating the garage was built sometime after 1903 (but before 1917).

The garage floor, as was the basement floor, was hard-packed dirt.  Dark patches in the dirt gave notice of oil leaking from car engines.

The garage originally was a one-cottage-type affair that accommodated a single car.  Dad built a lean-to addition on the east side of the garage to berth a second automobile.  The cottage had a heavy but manageable garage door made of vertical, wooden panels.  This articulated door hung by rollers on a rail.  By design, the cottage door accordioned open by sliding toward the right to neatly tuck against the west wall.

What whiz redesigned garage doors with horizontal panels, so that the doors rolled up overhead and out of the way? In 1921, C.G. Johnson invented the upward-lifting garage door. When our garage was open, Dad's tools hanging on that part of the west wall were inaccessible. In fact, when working in the garage, Dad opened the door only halfway, for easy access to his tools.

The lean-to had a different configuration. It had a pair of doors that opened outward from the center. These small doors dragged along the ground. (The sliding door on its track was easier to maneuver.)

Dad's diverse assortment of tools was impressive when displayed inside the garage. His small tools hung neatly from the walls, large ones occupied the floor and tools in use were spread out on his workbenches. The benches spanned the entire length of the south wall. Another workbench extended half way on the west side of the garage to leave room for the sliding door. The workbenches were about three and a half foot off the floor and about two foot deep.

Dad installed these workbenches himself.

Beneath the workbenches he stored equipment. There he kept rolls of electrical wire, kegs of nails, galvanized one-inch pipes (and other diameters), rolls of barb wire, heavy-duty jacks for raising up buildings, old tires, gasoline cans and kerosene cans.

On jobs, Dad took along a portable toolbox with a rope handle. He put in only tools he needed for any particular job on any particular day.

A chest full of tools sat on the floor on the west wall where the workbench ended. The chest was a converted steamer trunk-- old, squared off and painted black. Inside was a removable tray, perfect for storing small hand tools. Underneath this tray was storage for heavier or longer tools. Dad hand lettered (on the lid and on countless surfaces everywhere) in bright white paint:

## B. E. WOOLF

The workbench enchanted a 10-year-old (me) with an 8-year-old baby brother in tow and he was a baby. When we grew bored teasing Mr. Stratton's bull, we frequented our garage. Homer and I picked up Dad's tools, loving the heft of them. Dad unselfishly (to a certain degree) allowed us to play with his tools. Homer and I were fascinated by these implements, especially Dad's levels, handsome instruments that they were. We mock-used his hand drills, levels, wood-shaving planes, chisels, coping saws, T squares of all sizes-- among Dad's various tools. We attempted to build a variety of projects with the tools but I cannot remember a single project—picking up Dad's tools to emulate him was fun.

Perhaps he let us play with his prized tools because of this flattery. For us kids, it was sheer privilege.

"Marcell," Dad said often enough before supper, "What did I tell you about putting the tools up?"

"Um-m, you said to put them back where they belong," I said. I looked down at the comic book I'd been reading and wondered where Homer had disappeared to.

"Then go do it now," Dad said. "If you can't put them back where they belong then don't get 'em out in the first place. Do ya understand?"

"Ye-es," I said. I grabbed Homer as he reappeared from the kitchen. We scuttled out to the garage to rid up the tools. We were so convinced Dad meant business, we tidied up the garage into better shape than we'd found it.

*I* GUESS IT TOOK BECAUSE THIS PAST YEAR, WHEN INSTALLING A STORM DOOR, I PUT THE HAND TOOLS AWAY THREE TIMES BEFORE MY DO-IT-*YERSELF* JOB WAS DONE.

Speaking of "Dad meaning business," another item brought stern attention. A cardboard box sat menacingly on Dad's tool bench, beneath the window overlooking the privy. This container, bearing a sizeable picture of a skull and crossbones, was labeled **PARIS GREEN** --the box was the size of a modern, one-pound box of baking soda, about 6 inches high by 5 inches wide by 2 inches deep.

"Don't ever, EVER, touch that box," Dad warned us often enough. "It is poison." For once, we obeyed. We knew Dad meant business. He used this rodenticide to kill rats in the barn. Several times a month, Dad took the entire box up the hill to pour some powder into rat holes inside the barn. Rats perceived the barn for what it was in the rodent world: a free smörgåsbord. The barn was well stocked with a variety of grains (oats or wheat and always corn for the hens). These rats were bold. They came out of their holes during daylight and brazenly mocked us, *whitching* their *twiskers* at us. We kids spotted their comings and goings by their goings (droppings) on the floor near their nests, marked by telltale holes gnawed in wooden planks. Rodents had the run of the place scurrying in-between the floor joists.

Paris Green (so named because Parisians used this dye to exterminate rats in city sewers) contains arsenic. It was commercially used as a (rather deadly) clothing dye and as a paint pigment (a popular shade of green). When that box in our garage was finished, Dad never bought another. I think he felt it was just too dangerous to have around kids.

---

*P*IGMENTS SUCH AS PARIS GREEN HAVE BEEN IMPLICATED IN DISORDERS SUFFERED BY IMPRESSIONIST ARTISTS, E.G. MONET AND VAN GOGH, WHO MIXED THEIR OWN OIL PAINTS USING (IN IGNORANCE) TOXIC CHEMICAL COMPOUNDS. THESE CONDITIONS INCLUDED MENTAL ILLNESS, BLINDNESS AND SEVERE DIABETES.

Dad was organized. Everything had its place. He used drawers, boxes, containers and baskets to stow various small tools and parts. A trio of vises in various sizes and strengths were anchored to the workbenches. Two vises sat in the southwest corner of the garage and the other sat near the center of the south wall. Dad used one of these vises to secure his saws for sharpening, to bend metal pipes or to cut pieces of wood.

Hanging on the west wall were saws (hacksaws, coping saws, rip-cutting and cross-cutting saws in graduated sizes), hand drills with little cranks, drill bits, awls, hammers (both claw and ball-peen), slotted-head screwdrivers of various sizes. [Phillips-head screws were invented in the early 1930's but I don't recall Dad having Phillips screwdrivers back then.]`

There were pliers of all kinds— needle-nosed, slip joint pliers, pincers (we called these "pinchers"); wrenches of all sorts— pipe wrenches, adjustable-end wrenches, monkey wrenches; open-end and box-end wrenches (or combinations thereof); big folding knives; brads and various nails, including roofing nails; screws of all sizes; bolts and nuts; washers, grommets, cork for cushioning metal surfaces in contact with each other; and shears for cutting metal—we called them "tin snips."

Electric drills and other electrical hand tools had been invented but my dad didn't have any in the 1930's.

In addition to Dad's workshop, the garage housed our cars as makes, models and *marques* changed over the years.

In 1934 I was 10 years old. My dad was 48. "B.E.," as Dad referred to himself, was six foot tall.

"Jake," someone invariably asked, "how tall are you?"

"Five foot twelve," he replied, with dead-pan ease.

Dad had straight, dark brown hair and brown eyes. He had big ears. He really did have big ears. Dad parted his hair on the left side and combed it over. When he died at age 98, Dad still had a full shock of hair and big ears. Florence and Homer (on either end) inherited Dad's brown eyes, and everyone in the middle got Mother's precious blue eyes, including yours truly.

Dad's cronies at the Lodge Hall nicknamed him "Jake." But none of us kids or Mother ever called him that. Dad had a richly cultivated sense of humor. He loved playing tricks and practical jokes on people and never missed an opportunity to pull someone's leg. He would glue a silver dollar to a floor then laugh at anyone and everyone who tried vainly to pick it up.

"Come back again when you can't stay so long," he said to unwitting visitors at the house. Most of them didn't even catch this quip. They were not paying close attention and no doubt heard instead, "Come back when you can stay longer" (thank goodness).

Byron was a hard worker and expected his wife and children to pull their weight too. He was innovative. Dad's stance was that every problem had a solution and somehow knew how to set about finding it— a fortunate combination of optimism, innovativeness and deduction. He was truly ingenious. Although we didn't have an indoor flush-type toilet, Dad was the one who got the idea to convert the original pantry off the kitchen into a bathroom. Sumner Stanley might have been a carpenter but it was my dad who followed through to install the only bathroom in the house. (Now I must wonder where in the devil Sumner's family bathed. I'm picturing his wife washing up at the kitchen sink or using a pitcher and bowl. And shaving-- Sumner, not his wife-- did he shave at the kitchen sink!)

Maybe he had a long beard.

Until 1929, Dad worked as a carpenter for the Pennsylvania Railroad. An argument with a job boss and aftershocks of the New York stock market implosion that reached into northeast Ohio caught up with Dad. The contrast between the mid-20's building boom and Depression-era Ohio was gruesome. Carpentry jobs, especially freelance jobs attractive to Dad, dried up.

One negative effect of the Depression was a cash shortage on our farm. Somehow Dad got the *Pullet-zer* Prize-winning notion to start a pullet farm on the scale of 200 hens. Was this suggested to him by someone? I'd like to think it was Dad's or Mother's original idea. Priorly, as mentioned, we always had about 10 chickens scratching in the yard, providing eggs only for our immediate family and not for sale. There had never been any thought of our selling eggs before. Neighbor families raised perhaps 15 or 20 chickens for their own use too but there were no other chicken farms in our neck of the woods. Why hadn't anyone done it before? The nearest outfit was down in Columbiana County, 20 miles south.

What a brainstorm! We began farming eggs when everyone else in the environs was farming dairy.

Fellow carpenters had taught Dad the rudiments of indoor "finish carpentry" in home construction. From this on-the-job training, Dad learned how to install staircases, baseboards, flooring, paneling, door jambs, window casements— all the finish-out work. He was capable of building kitchen cabinets but contractors utilized cabinetmakers for that task. For the remainder of his life, Byron worked on and off at carpentry.

Dad also built furniture. He made a solid coffee table out of dark walnut for our living room; all the stands for Mother's indoor plants; the hall tree, tool boxes and shelving. He hammered nails into the walls if he was bored. Dad made a table for Mother's egg-candling operation in the basement and for her washtub stand.

A positive effect of the Depression was that it motivated Dad to expand his carpentry repertoire from indoor finishing to out-building. Before launching our poultry business, Dad needed to design and build appropriate housing— the only structures on our 16 acres had been our house, garage, privy and barn. A laying house had to be built and my dad was the man for the job. He had help but it was his bailiwick. Dad was also versatile enough to extend wiring from our house, in order to electrify the laying house (once erected) and the barn.

Meanwhile, from a New Jersey hatchery, mail-order baby chicks were on the way and Dad was almost on his way. He needed someplace to put the new chicks. He really scrambled to find room for them.

Well: what came first, the egg or the chicken? Do you want me to answer that? In this case, the chicken came first— we didn't have any eggs! With limited space, Dad chose the barn to carve out a brooder house to shelter this initial order of baby chicks. By the time the laying house was finished and furnished, the baby chicks were not chicks anymore. They had grown into laying hens ready for transfer to the laying house.

After Dad walked off his railroad job, he had a sense of urgency about getting his poultry venture up and running. His efforts generated cash only after the peeps grew up and started laying— roughly six months. So he was juggling two projects simultaneously: building the laying house for the adult chickens and caring for the newly arrived baby chicks in the barn.

Thus, my dad's know-how allowed him to know how to lay the infrastructure of a prospering chicken farm in 1930-- from scratch-- with the weight of the Great Depression beginning to bear down on our family.

My father's temperament was fairly even. He lost his temper at times when he was provoked beyond his limit. We children (sort of) knew what his limits were. He was a man to say what he meant and he meant what he said. His word was not to be disputed, by my mother or by us six kids. But Dad was not a brute.

I never heard Dad and Mother arguing with or yelling at each other. He treated us kids fairly by avoiding playing favorites.

A good provider, Dad was friendly to the neighbors (excluding the Roepkes and the Boyds). Above all, he was honest and scrupulous in his business dealings. Later, in the course of my work as a registered nurse, I was exposed to a new phenomenon: a breed of adults who lied through their teeth. It was only then I fully appreciated how honest Dad was.

I loved my dad but never physically demonstrated it, nor did he hug us or pat us on the back when we did a good job. We didn't exchange outward demonstrations of affection.

Dad was a good sport. He allowed Homer and me to accompany him on errands. We didn't have a (pick-up) truck. Dad had built a trailer for hauling feed and lumber. This trailer attached to our family car. On trips to the feed mill, Dad and the owner, Richard Hawkins, loaded the trailer with 50-pound sacks of chicken mash. While they labored, Homer and I labored at dashing around the spacious interior of the mill, causing a general stir and a specific embarrassment to my dad. He also let us tag along on visits to his folks' house, to other farmers' operations up and down Route 534, and on trips to Alliance to pick up a load of lumber or to Salem to buy plumbing and wiring supplies.

Maybe Dad enjoyed Homer's and my company. Going places with Dad was fun, especially considering we always invited our *impudinent* selves to go along.

# VIGNETTE: GOES HAND IN HAND.

EVERY SPRING AND FALL, SEARS, ROEBUCK & COMPANY MAILED OUT A NEW CATALOGUE. ALL OF US WOOLFS EAGERLY ANTICIPATED THIS BIANNUAL OCCASION. IT WAS A BIG DEAL.

ONCE THE NEW CATALOGUE WAS IN HAND, THE OUTDATED ONE WAS HANDED OVER TO THE OUTHOUSE, HANDILY CALLED "THE TOILET." MY EVER-HANDY FATHER DRILLED A HOLE IN THE CATALOGUE, AT THE TOP NEAR THE SPINE. THROUGH THIS HOLE, HE PASSED A LENGTH OF TWINE TO HANG THE CATALOGUE FROM A NAIL ON THE WEST WALL OF THE PRIVY. THIS STOOD-IN HANDSOMELY FOR A ROLL OF TOILET PAPER. WE DIDN'T HAVE CHARMIN OR ANYTHING TO COMPARE IT TO. AT LEAST IT WAS SOFTER THAN BUTCHER PAPER, WHICH WAS BROWN, CRINKLY, HARSH TO THE TOUCH AND HEAVY.

THE PAGES IN THE CATALOGUE WERE THIN AS TISSUE. JUST LIKE TISSUE PAPER— NOT AS SOFT AS KLEENEX BUT CLOSE TO THE TEXTURE OF MODERN TELEPHONE-DIRECTORY PAGES. THEY WERE WONDERFUL TO WIPE WITH. IN THE 1930's, SEARS INTRODUCED CLAY-COATED, FULL-COLOR CATALOGUES. THIS TRAVESTY CAUSED AN UPROAR. CITIZENS ACROSS THE LAND COMPLAINED TO SEARS THAT THE NEW PAPER WAS STIFF AND NO LONGER ABSORBENT FOR CERTAIN UNMENTIONABLE PURPOSES.

ALL THE NEIGHBORS USED THE SEARS CATALOGUE AS TOILET PAPER. IT WAS A SITTING—ER, STANDING JOKE. SEARS CATALOGUE PAGES NOT ONLY SERVED AS TOILET PAPER BUT DOUBLED AS ENTERTAINING READING MATERIAL WHILE SITTING ON THE HOLE BEFORE ONE NEEDED TO USE THEM.

# CHAPTER 14:
## THE KITCHEN GARDEN:
## VEGETABLES GROWN FOR THE TABLE.

*"DON'T EAT TOO MANY CUCUMBERS*
*OR YOU'LL GET CHOLERY MORBUS."*

--DAD

OUR farm produced nearly all the food that wound up on our table and the forage that fed our animals. Willow Run Farm provided sustenance for our family of eight and for our pigs, our dairy cow and our chickens, during all seasons.

Willow Run made it possible for us to survive the Depression with dignity.

We grew a modicum of fruit on the farm and plenty of vegetables in a kitchen garden; kept a dairy cow for milk, cream, butter, buttermilk and *schmearkase* (GERMAN: "cottage cheese"); raised chickens for eggs and Sunday dinner; and pigs for bacon, ham and sausage.

The first item in this roster (the fruit and the kitchen garden) is the theme for this chapter. Animal husbandry is reserved for the second volume of this trilogy, a book encompassing the period 1935 to 1941.

Of Willow Run's 16 acres of farmland, we apportioned six to potatoes and forage crops. We rotated alfalfa and clover hay, field corn, wheat and oats. These cultivable grasses we raised solely to feed our Jersey cow, a dozen or so white pigs and our chickens. As discussed, before Willow Run Farm became "Willow Run Poultry Farm" in 1930 or '31, our family kept some 10 chickens scratching around the back yard. Yet at the height of its productivity in the 1940's, our farm husbanded upwards of 1,500 chickens.

Our kitchen garden was a one-sixteenth-acre plot. Its dimensions were about 30 foot along the driveway by 90 foot parallel to Route 534. The plot was located just east of the garage and across the drive from the house. From 534 to the garden, the driveway ran relatively flat, then steeply uphill (from west to east). However, the garden sloped gently downhill away from the garage (from west to east also).

Such are the idiosyncrasies of glaciated land in northeast Ohio, where farms and parklands bear scars from the ice ages. Debris, ranging in size from boulders to rocks to gravel, embedded itself in the underbelly of glacial floes, creating sandpaper on a monstrous scale. The gritty mass scoured the terrain into irregular troughs and undulations as the ice advanced and retreated. The uphill-downhill-uphill landscape of Willow Run provided a modern snapshot of events that occurred in Ohio as recently as 15,000 years ago. The power of glacial ice to polish-- or gouge out-- a landscape on a caprice is formidable. (A carpenter who mis-applies coarse 40-grit sandpaper to a fine wooden antique and corrects the mistake by working up to super-fine 800-grit appreciates this effect.)

Our farmscape was as helter-skelter as the chunk of land Mill Creek School was plunked down on.

THE RIVULATIONS AT WILLOW RUN WERE A MINOR AFFAIR COMPARED TO A MORE-SIZEABLE FOOTPRINT GLACIERS LEFT 60 MILES NORTH OF OUR FARM: LAKE ERIE.

The plot where we gardened was the most plausible venue on the property: handy to the house, in full sun and fairly flat. Whoever carved out the plot originally— Sumner Stanley or my dad— did an admirable job of selecting the most level site within watermelon-seed-spitting distance of the house. Despite its slight slope, the garden layout was flat enough for us to cultivate vegetables.

Each April, Dad plowed this area for Mother. His homemade tractor was ingenious. With it, he pulled a double-bladed steel plow on metal wheels.

Following the plowing, Dad returned to the garden with a harrow, also pulled behind the tractor. Dad had bought this harrow at a farm sale. Certainly he got it for a good price because if he hadn't he wouldn't have bought it. It did not have wheels but lay flat against the earth. It looked like a set of bedsprings with railroad spikes protruding evenly throughout, pointed tips facing Chinaward. Maybe five rows and seven crossbars comprised the grid of the harrow. This contraption broke up large clods of dirt cast aside earlier by the plow.

Once prepared by plowing and harrowing, the garden was ready for planting. We all had to dig in. All of us kids mildly dreaded the coming of late April or early May. Planting was a tiresome chore but could not be described as a harrowing experience. We whined a lot to my mother, although we looked forward to the fruits of our labors at harvest time (rather, the vegetables of our labor).

In the end, it was a labor of love.

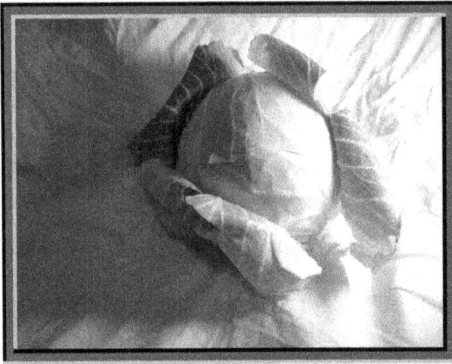

While Dad readied the plot, Mother made a list of progenitors for her garden. Every spring, Dad made his annual pilgrimage to Mecca with list in hand--his destination not Mecca, Ohio, but LaRue Hawkins General Store in Berlin Center. Dad bought seeds and starter plants (we called them "starts") for cabbage, onions and tomatoes.

Starts were plants just too difficult to grow from seed. Long winters in northeast Ohio abbreviated our growing season. For the corn and potatoes we grew, we used our own stock. We had to buy packets of seed for the remainder of garden vegetables we raised.

From east to west, we laid out the vegetables in rows parallel to Route 534, except for the rhubarb patch.

The layout was as follows: corn, cucumbers, squash, beans, cabbage, tomatoes (all in full rows); and radish, chard, beets, snap peas, kohlrabi, onions and carrots in half rows. Rhubarb grew along the south edge, at a 90-degree angle to the rest of the rows.

The corn that grew along the entire east edge of the kitchen garden was sweet corn and it was succulent. For the planting in May, Mother dug (with a hoe) a small hole, no more than two or three inches deep. In bare feet, one of us children walked behind her to drop three kernels of specially aged hard corn into the hole. No more, no less—we counted out the kernels as we walked along. Then, Mother doubled back to cover the holes. She gently feathered dirt with the tip of her hoe to cap the kernels within their hole.

To prepare corn for seed, let's look at the process. The seed came from our own garden, year after year, employing last season's crop. By late August, fresh corn on the cob for table use had been depleted. Sweet corn has a short window of palatability, its season three weeks or longer. Into September, ears remaining on the stalks (thus unsuitable for the table) were destined for use as dried corn or as seed corn.

Corn destined for drying was put up eventually in jars, for later consumption—this dried corn provided welcome side dishes to allay monotonous winter suppers.

Corn destined for seed was shucked of its husks in late September and stored all winter on the cob, in a basket beside the kitchen stove. The following May, we shelled this corn, then put it in a small sack. We saved the cobs for the pigs. That is how we prepared seed corn for germinating.

The east border of the garden was given over to three full rows of this sweet corn, mouth-wateringly nick-named "bread and butter corn" for its speckling of white kernels and yellow kernels. Sweet corn was ripe for picking starting in the second week of August. For three or four weeks, our dinner table was graced with heaping platters of fresh, boiled corn on the cob. Mother served it lavishly spread with her homemade, salted butter.

A-maize-ing. ¡*Vive Zea mays*! (Genus/species, *corn*).

---

**W**E HAD EARS OF CORN COMING OUT OUR EARS.

---

For nearly a month, we ate our fill. Thereafter, the indescribable taste of truly fresh (not store-bought) sweet corn was a memory until the following year.

Meanwhile, we had rows of perfectly-good corn we had to leave standing on the stalk-- maturing, then desiccating, generally growing more tough and less tasty day after day as the sugars converted to starch—

increasingly limited how much fresh corn we could consume.

To preserve this excess corn we couldn't consume, Mother dried it or saved it for next season's seed, as noted.

Alongside the corn, we planted cucumbers by seed also. Throughout the summer, Mother prepared various-sized pickles by selecting various-sized cucumbers. (Wee pickles are not made from humongous cucumbers, as commonly thought. What you pick from the garden is what you get. Pickling does not shrink a cucumber.) As summer wore on, Mother put up, in this order: gherkins, bread-and-butter pickles, then dill pickles.

We raised long, yellow summer squash. We didn't know about zucchini-- we were not acquainted with that type of squash. We also raised a winter variety, acorn squash.

---

THE CUCUMBER AND SQUASH VINES INTERMINGLED PROFLIGATELY IN THE GARDEN. THESE TYPES OF INDISCRETIONS HAPPEN ON A FARM.

---

We planted beans and peas in the same way as corn: Mother dug a hole and we dropped the beans in. Three seeds per hole. Again, no more no less. Beans and snap peas were among the vegetables whose seed Dad had to purchase at Hawkins General Store. One full row of green beans lay alongside the squash. A second row of beans went in next, an entire row of limas.

The beanstalks had to be tied to sticks. For these, we broke branches off a locust tree in a grove east of the garden. The grove was on the way up the hill to the barn. We stuck the locust sticks in the ground next to the bean plants. We tied a string around beanstalk and stick alike, put in a few knots, and the plant was staked.

This practice was rooted in sound agricultural theory to diminish problems with rot, worms and infest insectations that threatened to strip a plant nearly overnight.

Next came our two garden staples: cabbage and tomatoes. We raised both from the young starts Dad bought at the General Store. About eight inches tall, the cabbages were fast growers and grew fat as oysters.

Homer and I were capable of lending a hand to help plant corn and beans, which involved simply dropping a trio of seeds into a hole. However, three of my older siblings-- Elaine, Doris and Delmus-- got themselves volunteered to handle the cabbage, tomato and onion starts. The starts had to be set straight up into a deep hole. Then a cup of water had to be poured at the base; with the dirt replaced and patted down to firm the roots-- all the while keeping the plant upright to protect the frail stems from snapping in half. Surely this was not a job for a youngster. Besides, I always felt my talents were better put to use chasing Homer up and down the rows while everyone else labored.

In the kitchen, Mother put a humble cabbage to noble use by making cole slaw or sauerkraut, or by serving cabbage fried or boiled with ham.

> " *T*HE TIME HAS COME," THE WALRUS SAID,
> "TO TALK OF MANY THINGS:
> OF SHOES --AND SHIPS--AND SEALING-WAX--
> O F CABBAGES--AND KINGS--
> AND WHY THE SEA IS BOILING HOT--
> AND WHETHER PIGS HAVE WINGS."
>
> --LEWIS CARROLL
> *THE WALRUS AND THE CARPENTER*

We raised tomatoes by the bushel. We didn't grow cherry or plum tomatoes, only the beefsteak variety. The tomato stalks had to be staked like the beans. Should they be named "beefstake" tomatoes instead? One beefsteak tomato might weigh in at more than a pound.

These were no agribidness fabrications. Our tomatoes were red inside and red outside and red in between; sweet, sloppy, soft and so plump they begged to be squeezed.

They were real tomatoes.

The planting was uninspiring for a tomboy like me (who preferred chasing Homer around the yard) but certainly it was not grueling work-- just kinda tedious. Mother helped us make a game of planting by counting the kernels or seeds or starts and singing as we sowed. Perhaps she sewed as she sang too.

The west edge of the garden lay no more than eight feet from the lean-to addition to the garage. The three final rows were split in half by a strip of Mother's marigolds. In the north section of half-rows were radishes, Swiss chard, beets and snap peas. The south section's half was kohlrabi, big fat white onions and carrots. These half-dozen vegetables grew well from seed in our short growing season. Onions got their start from bulbs we bought.

Mother read the Farm & Dairy journal prodigiously. She knew the value of apportioning the kitchen garden toward a balance of food which had one of three destinations:

- eating fresh (in season)
- dry- or wet-curing
- cool-storing

The first category included vegetables grown as pure indulgence. Snap peas, Swiss chard and summer squash were fragile and could not be canned or otherwise stored appropriately. They had to be eaten upon ripening, either by people or by the porcine elements. Of course, for the Woolf family, the obligation to eat the snap peas snappily, for one—well, no hardship. Ambrosial.

We let the carrots grow to full size. We didn't pull them up early to eat "baby carrots." We grew good red radishes and white radishes. The rows of radishes were short, about thirty feet—still an awful lot of radishes! I love a sandwich with red radishes, real tomatoes, sweet onions and chunky peanut butter when I can find decent bread.

Our beets got as big as tennis balls. They were good. Just like radishes and carrots, beets are true root vegetables of the taproot type. These three half-rows occupied about one-tenth of the garden's real estate. Mother devoted space to root vegetables because they lasted through winter without any fuss— no drying, no canning, no pickling, no curing.

In addition to beets, we grew an off-beat vegetable, kohlrabi, a type of cabbage. The name derives from the German, *kohl* ("cabbage") and *rabi* ("turnip"). The up beat is— it was an unbeatable snack. We yanked a kohlrabi out of the ground, washed it off and pared the kohlrabi like a potato to remove the root and little sprouts. We ate kohlrabies raw, peppered with salt but not salted with pepper. Raw, they taste like... well... cabbage.

We never cooked kohlrabi. When cooked, they taste like cauliflower.

From store-bought bulbs, we grew softball-sized white onions. When ready to pick, long green tops protruded above the ground. The onions had to be dug out of the dirt. They are underground vegetables of the bulb type, not true root vegetables.

ONIONS WERE A MAINSTAY. MOTHER ADDED ONIONS TO EVERYTHING EXCEPT QUAKER OATMEAL AND BAKED CUSTARD. SHOULD IT COME AS A SURPRISE THAT I ENJOY A GOOD PEANUT-BUTTER-AND-ONION SANDWICH TODAY?

'Midships, along the south border of the garden, at the end of the cabbage and tomato rows, we grew rhubarb for condiments and pies. "Rhubarb" comes from words meaning "foreign rhubarb."

We never raised the following: broccoli, cantaloupe, cauliflower, celery, garlic, kale, lettuce, parsnips, bell peppers, sweet potatoes, turnips or yams.

Nice if we'd a grown sweet potatoes and yams!

We never had salads. We did not have olive oil to put on salads. Lettuce was too frail a target for insects, and rabbits, raccoons and other unwelcome nocturnal snackers. In hindsight and to Mother's credit, what she chose to grow in the kitchen garden was hearty stock. Lettuce and other *fragilables* meshed poorly with that plan, deliberate planning on Mother's part. Actually it is quite amazing, taking it all in.

---

*I*N OUR GARDEN, MOTHER PLANTED MARIGOLDS IN-BETWEEN THE SHORT HALF-ROWS TO KEEP RABBITS OUT BUT THE BUNNIES CAME ANYWAY AND ATE THEIR FILL.
THAT'S WHY WE DIDN'T GROW LETTUCE.
THE RABBITS EVEN ATE THE MARIGOLDS.

---

During summer, Dodie, Elaine and I had to weed the garden by hand. The rows were too narrow for Dad to run the tractor-cultivator combo through. Dem dare dam weeds never let up! It was a job no one liked. In fact, we all hated weeding, but we were glad of *dem* vegetables later. On hot days, we had to water the tomatoes and cabbage plants by hand. We used a bucket of water filled from an outside spicket and used a dipper to give them a bit of relief from the heat. We had neither a hose nor enough water in the well to douse the plants but good.

We relied on the benevolence of rainfall.

We planted white potatoes in a plot east of the house, across the driveway from the vegetable garden. Potatoes are tubers, not true root vegetables, but they stored well over the winter. Dad had a six-acre planting field that ran north of the house, along 534 and past the corner of Western Reserve Road. He reserved a portion of this acreage for the potatoes. He also plowed and harrowed this acreage for rotation crops— alfalfa, clover hay, field corn, wheat and oats for fodder or for bedding for our livestock.

For potato propagation, we used the vegetative method. In May, Mother had to sort out potato starters from bags stored the winter prior. She selected potatoes with prominent eyes-- sprouts and roots already about a half-inch long. When planting time rolled around, she cut starters, ensuring each chunk had one or two eyeable vies (I mean, viable eyes).

For the 'tater planting, three of us kids were out there helping Dad. Using a trailer towed by his homespun tractor, Dad loaded the sacks of starters that Mother had sorted and cut into pieces. He hauled the sacks to the potato plot. For the actual planting, Dad dug up a shovel full of dirt. One of us traipsing behind him dropped in a potato portion. Delmus trundled behind our crew and covered the hole with a hoe.

The starters grew rapidly once in the ground. Soon potato sprouts broke through the soil.

*I*NDEED, THE HIGH ADAPTABILITY OF THE LOWLY POTATO IN POOR TERRAIN LED TO WIDESPREAD PLANTING IN IRELAND, MID-1800'S, ALL EGGS INTO ONE BASKET. THIS VIRTUAL MONOCULTURE WAS RIPE FOR DISASTER. BLIGHT SWEPT THROUGH. THIS *CULTIVATED* FAMINE RESULTED IN A DEATH TOLL OF ONE MILLION IRISH.

The potatoes also required heavy weeding. We had to be more aggressive in weeding than the weeds were in growing. We had to stay on top of it. Dad used the cultivator behind his tractor to take care of the weeds in this plot-- the potato plants were less delicate and the furrows wider than in the kitchen garden.

In the fall we had the task of pulling potatoes. It was Delmus's job to dig up the mature potatoes with a heavy-duty digging fork. This was not a pitchfork. Each plant, quite bushy topside, produced six or eight potatoes underground. Delmus shook each clump vigorously to rid them of dirt and went on to the next one. Our job was to put the potatoes into rugged burlap bags after pulling them away from the green tops. That took some exertion.

We did this chore after we came home from school-- it was that far into the season, late September. We hurried to get it done, as pulling potatoes involved a lot of leaning over and lifting. And it could still be quite warm in northeast Ohio that time of year. The discarded greenery got carried up the hill to the pig house.

Everyone except Mother harvested potatoes.

We loaded 10 to 15 burlap sacks to the bulging point with 50 to 80 pounds of these white potatoes. Dad delivered them via tractor-trailer to the south side of the house. We unloaded the sacks and stacked them by the cellar window. A team of us children remained behind as Dad hiked down to the fruit cellar. We handed the burlap sacks to him through the window. Dad placed the potatoes in proximity to the root vegetables (carrots, beets and radishes); and the onions, winter squash and pumpkins; and cabbages not earmarked for sauerkraut.

"I eat watermelon 'cuz it wets my ears," we sang.

---

OH I EAT WATERMELON AND I HAVE FOR YEARS, SING POLLY WOLLY DOODLE ALL THE DAY. I LIKE WATERMELON BUT IT WETS MY EARS. SING POLLY WOLLY DOODLE ALL THE DAY.

--S. CLARE & B. DESYLVA
"POLLY WOLLY DOODLE"

Dad loved watermelon. We tried to grow a few for him between the rows of cornstalks near the north side of the house.   Our summers were not consistently hot enough. The watermelons came up stunted.  They never matured-- just not hot enough for long enough in our corner of the Buckeye State, beautiful Ohio.

Near the watermelon, we were able to grow barn-sized pumpkins (not that big, but they were big).  They grew in-between the rows of field corn.  We only grew a few pumpkins because Mother did not "can" pumpkins. She just used them fresh, for buttery-smooth pumpkin pies.  One pumpkin went a *lonnnng* way.

Our focus now turns away from the kitchen garden to the kitchen, where Mother's canning operation was already in full swing as we harvested potatoes.

What we could eat fresh we ate, but what we couldn't eat fresh we had to preserve in some fashion, by canning, drying, fermenting, curing or putting up for cool storage in the cellar.  Mother spent four months of the year conserving food for the other eight months of idle garden time. This labor allowed our family to feed ourselves throughout an entire year.

# VIGNETTE: REST IN PEACE.

ONE SUMMER DAY DAD HAD COME HOME FROM WORK. WE KIDS INNOCENTLY SQUEALED ON DELMUS, WHO HAD BEEN TEASING LAEG, OUR GERMAN SHEPHERD. THE DOG HAD BIT DELMUS. DAD HAD BECOME ENRAGED. NOT JUST AT LAEG, BUT AT ALL OF US CHILDREN.

A FEW WEEKS LATER, DELMUS TOLD DAD THAT LAEG HAD KILLED AND EATEN A CHICKEN. DAD LET THIS GO. HE DIDN'T DO ANYTHING AT THE TIME (EVEN THOUGH IT WAS KNOWN COMMONLY THAT AN ANIMAL THAT KILLS WILL DO SO AGAIN, MOST LIKELY). SEVERAL DAYS LATER, LAEG KILLED AND ATE ANOTHER CHICKEN. I CANNOT IMAGINE HOW CHICKENS GOT NEAR THE DOG HOUSE, BECAUSE THE CHICKENS WERE KEPT IN THE LAYING HOUSE AND LAEG WAS ALWAYS CHAINED TO HIS DOGHOUSE. A FEW DAYS LATER, LAEG KILLED AND ATE A THIRD CHICKEN. DELMUS TOLD DAD. THIS TIME DAD REALLY LOST HIS TEMPER. HE MARCHED UP TO THE DOG HOUSE. HE SEIZED A TWO-BY-FOUR THAT WAS LAYING THERE AND BEGAN TO BEAT THE DOG ABOUT THE HEAD. MOTHER CAME OUT OF THE HOUSE WHEN SHE HEARD LAEG HOWLING. FROM THE BOTTOM OF THE BARN HILL, MOTHER, HOMER, ELAINE, DODIE AND I WITNESSED THIS SCENE. LAEG WAS CHAINED THE ENTIRE TIME AND MY DAD BEAT LAEG UNTIL THE DOG WAS DEAD. MOTHER AND WE CHILDREN DID NOT DARE BREATHE A WORD OF PROTEST TO DAD.

DAD AND DELMUS COOLY BURIED OUR WATCHDOG, DEAR LAEG. NO ONE EVER CONFRONTED MY FATHER ABOUT THIS LATER. WE JUST DID NOT DARE INTERFERE. THE SUBJECT WAS NEVER RAISED. IT WAS NEVER DISCUSSED.

--C. 1931

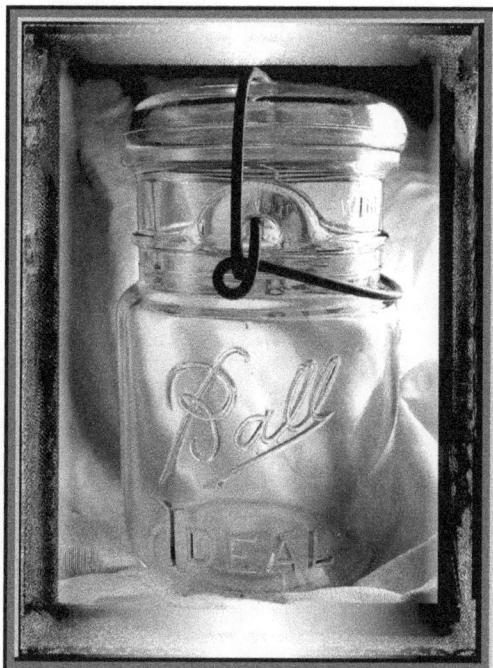

# CHAPTER 15:
## FOOD PRESERVING.

*"WE EAT WHAT WE CAN AND
WHAT WE CAN'T EAT WE CAN."*

--DAD

*m*OTHER'S domain was the kitchen. She worked hard in her corner of the world. She not only provided three wholesome meals for the eight or so of us, every and each day, but also did it without modern conveniences that make household duties less toilsome.

She went about her duties without complaint.

Most of the farm families in our circumjacencies worked hard. Mother was no Sam Weingart sitting around waiting for a Relief check. From the time she put up the breakfast dishes until she put up the supper dishes, Mother never took much pause to put up her feet.

Our growing season in northeast Ohio was ±150 days. Our five-month season was the second shortest in the entire state, i.e., nearly the coldest.

*I*SOTHERMS ARE LINES OF EQUAL TEMPERATURE DEPICTED ON MAPS TO INDICATE GROWING-SEASON DAYS OR FROST-FREE PERIODS-- AKIN TO THERMOCLINES INDICATING OCEAN-TEMPERATURE STRATA. IN OHIO, THE LOWEST, COLDEST ISOTHERM OF 140 DAYS OVERLAPS PORTIONS OF TRUMBULL, MAHONING AND COLUMBIANA COUNTIES JUST EAST OF OUR FARM. THE WARMEST GROWING SEASON, 200 DAYS, WRAPS AROUND CLEVELAND LIKE A SADDLE, CREATED BY LAKE ERIE'S "LAKE EFFECT." THIS MAKES SENSE-- ALL ALONG THE TURNPIKE BEYOND CLEVELAND, WEST TOWARD TOLEDO, ARE VAST FIELDS OF TOMATO PLANTS WHOSE PROGENY MIGHT BE DESTINED FOR HUNT OR HEINZ CANNING PLANTS. THOSE CHEEKY CLEVELANDERS ENJOYED AN ENTIRE 50 MORE FREEZELESS DAYS ANNUALLY EVEN THOUGH JUST 60 MILES NORTH OF US. I WONDER IF THEY SPRINKLE WHITE FLOUR ON THE TOMATO PLANTS TO KEEP BUGS OFF, AS MOTHER DID EVERY SUMMER.

Thus was our farm smack in the middle of the coldest region in Ohio. Our growing season lasted from mid-May or late May with the spring thaw, into late September or mid-October when the danger of frost returned with diminishing daylight.

THERMOCLINES ARE NO RELATION TO MY MOTHER'S FAMILY, THE HOMER CLINES OF BERLIN CENTER, OHIO.

Ohio's extreme-cold isotherm influenced our ability to grow (or not grow) crops-- for example, Dad's love of watermelon and our failed attempt to raise a crop (if you could call it that). It just wasn't hot enough. Our 10 or so stunted, permanently immature watermelons were plain white inside. What a disappointment. We never tried raising watermelons again.

THE POWER OF WEATHER TO SWAY CIRCUMSTANCE REMINDS ONE THAT STORMS (NOT SIR FRANCIS DRAKE) WRECKED THE SPANISH ARMADA IN 1588. ALONG WITH ANOTHER ODD FACT-- SUSTAINED FRIGID WEATHER PUT AN END TO ENGLISH VINEYARDS MID-15TH CENTURY. GRAPEVINES ONCE GREW PROLIFICALLY IN BRITAIN. WHO RECENTLY HAS HEARD OF BRITISH MERLOTS OR SCOTTISH CABERNET WINES? DO WATERMELONS GROW IN JOLLY OLDE?

In the spring, Mother busied herself planning and planting the vegetable garden.

In the summer, she tended the garden: pulling weeds, watering, picking early vegetables such as peas and small cucumbers, and trying to rid the garden of pests (like me and Homer). She followed her *in-stincks* by dusting her tomato plants with dry white flour to coat stink bugs and other insects. While struggling to clean the flour off themselves, the bugs fell to the ground. Mother may have learned this early version of crop dusting from her grandmother in the days before the inception of organic farming.

The timeframe from summer through fall is what this chapter is all about—the process of putting up produce as it matured. Fortunately, not every fruit or vegetable ripened at the same time. Were this true, Mother would've been overwhelmed to say the least. She was nearly overwhelmed anyway. Down time between laying-in the garden and laying up food was short. As early as June, e.g., she was canning peaches (grown by neighbors). In June, Mother's busy time really began. Her workload slackened toward late fall when corn was laid out for drying and our pumpkins were harvested.

Winters were time for Mother's leisure (if any). After the food we produced or procured was processed, she turned to her quilt making. Mother looked forward to the cold, short days of winter, to have the leisure to sit and sew or to retire early. For Mother, the task of quilting was one of her comforts and she was proud of the comforters she made— one blanket per year. Each bed upstairs displayed one of her handmade quilts.

Cast-off clothes were spared from the wastebasket and instead were stored in a wicker basket next to the sewing machine in Dad's room. When ready to begin a quilt, Mother selected the most colorful remnants or interesting patterns. She laid these on the library table and cut them into six-inch squares. First, she sewed four squares together to produce 12-inch squares. Each large square was then sewed onto a wool backing material she had bought from a dry goods store in Salem. The finished comforter bore about 120 six-inch squares all in all, surrounded by a border of unadorned backing. The top and bottom borders were 18 inches, the sides 12 inches.

Living on a farm during the Depression, without a refrigerator, without a deep freezer-- yet obliged to grow our own food— put us in a pickle. Resolving this dilemma fell to Mother. She had to figure out how to manage our kitchen-garden harvest efficiently. Only two options existed. What we couldn't eat fresh off the vine or couldn't conserve, went to waste. The waste we circumvented by raising pigs.

I focus now on the second option, the challenges we faced conserving a modest or even a bumper crop. (Any amateur gardener who ever planted a backyard full of green beans or a few rows of tomatoes knows whereof I speak. One can quickly get overrun.)

The point is that rural households had but a few weeks to dispose of produce that needed to produce variety for the table for an entire year.

Mother, having married at age 15, was forced to grow up fast. The duties of farm wifery required her to be a wizard of sorts. A domestic overseer, she had six methods at her disposal to preserve animal, vegetable and fruit products gleaned from our farm: drying, pickling, fermenting, canning, curing and cool-storage.

Any mention of "curing" (beyond Father Coughlin's paroxysms meant to cure the soul) is reserved for the second book in this trilogy, when pig husbandry on our farm is addressed. We will address each of the five remaining methods in succession herein.

None of these six methods involved refrigeration or freezing, unless we set something out on the back porch in winter! Surprisingly, Birds Eye frosted foods were available first in America in 1930. We never bought any. Even had frosted foods been available in our *purlieus*, we had no place to store them. We preserved our own.

*I*N THE LATE 1930'S, WE JOINED THE TWO-THIRDS OF AMERICAN HOUSEHOLDS THAT OWNED A REFRIGERATOR. UNTIL THAT TIME, WE HAD TO MAKE DO WITH OUR ICEBOX, WHICH HAD ROOM ONLY FOR THE MORNING OR EVENING MILK.

Our farm yielded a plethora of vegetables via the kitchen garden but a minim of fruit. Mother had to expand her repertoire by *preservatizing* fruits acquired elsewhere. We bartered for, bought or otherwise acquired fruits such as apples, bananas, cantaloupe (which we called "muskmelons"), blackberries, cherries, peaches, strawberries and watermelon. Oh! The watermelon, trucked up from Alabama or Georgia or someplace nice and *hot* (likely, not England).

For example: my family loved peaches. A thick slice of Mother's homemade peach pie or a thick slice of homemade bread with butter and her peach preserves was Mother setting her love on the table. We didn't grow our own peaches but bought them locally. Their availability made our life all the more— well, just peachy.

As a kid, I don't think I ever saw a lemon. My uncle Emerson (Dad's younger brother, the attorney, who gave my dad those hand-me-up suits) gave each of us children a gift of a navel orange at Christmas.

Big spender!

# VEGETABLE Conservation.

## DRYING VEGETABLES (CORN).

The sweet corn in our kitchen garden was ripe in late August. For three weeks, we enjoyed our fill at the supper table of sweet, fresh sweet corn. Talk about salivating!

Even after eating our fill of fresh corn, we had plenty left over. Mother made good use of this excess by putting up a few quarts of Chow Chow relish, then dried the remainder of what we couldn't eat. Recall the ears of corn coming out our ears?

Whether for eating or drying, we left the kitchen-garden corn on the stalk to mature. The bell marking the end of the sweet-corn-eating season tolled September 10th, give or take a week-- always sad to bid farewell to sweet-corn season.

Bread-and-butter corn was our bread and butter.

Mother and two or three of us younger girls carried empty bushel baskets to the garden. We filled the baskets with ears of corn too tough to eat. We shucked the ears at the back-porch steps while Mother hummed. We saved the corn husks and tassels for the pigs.

Mother parboiled the corn— on the cobs— in a substantial tinware kettle for not more than five minutes. The kettle was about 16 inches wide by 9 inches tall with a wire bailer and a lid. Mother set the ears out to cool on newspapers (ones my dad hadn't read yet) on the kitchen table.

Parboiling preserved the color and flavor of the corn kernels prior to drying. Native Americans preserved corn in this same fashion more than 2,000 years ago. I don't know how Mother learned this ancient technique. She read Grit magazine and farm journals or perhaps picked it up from her Mother or grandmother. Come to think of it, how did Indians figure out that briefly boiling corn before drying foiled rancidity and color loss? I find this all astonishing.

After the corn cooled, Mother removed the kernels. The spent cobs went to the pigs. The kernels were laid out on already-read newspapers in the closet in Dad's room. There the corn dried over a period of weeks.

When Mother sent me to retrieve something from that closet, I nicked a kernel or two of the drying corn to nibble on as a snack.

Later, Mother sealed the dehydrated kernels "dry," i.e., without salt, without liquid, in glass jars. These jars we stored in the fruit cellar on shelves, next to the green beans. Or maybe they were next to the lima beans.

Throughout a calendar year, until the next crop, Mother used this dried corn for cooking. She rehydrated it by warming the dried corn in a pan of water on the stove. She might have tossed in a chunk of butter for flavor. Mother mainly used the dried corn in succotash, an American dish common throughout the Depression. She made it by combining the reconstituted corn and her home-canned lima beans, with more chunks of butter and salt and pepper.

"Succotash" is derived from an American-Indian word meaning "mixed-together food." Ironically, the dish has been around for 2,000 years (or more), just as the method of parboiling corn prior to drying. Blanche Woolf dried corn and prepared succotash exactly as Indians did two millennia ago.

Quite un-*can*-ny!

# $V$EGETABLES WE CANNED.

We canned our homegrown vegetables. We bought seed for growing vegetables. We did not buy mature vegetables. That was the whole point. The wide variety of vegetables and fruits from our farm provided a horn-o'-plenty for our table around the calendar.

As stated, Mother was fortunate in that fruits and vegetables were seasonal, so she was not constantly canning. Produce ripened at different periods throughout the growing season. Late summer was her busiest time.

The fruit cellar reflected this abundance. Quarts of beets, green beans and lima beans lined the shelves down cellar alongside pint jars of jelly and carrots. The jars were many and varied. Just about the only items not put up in some way were such indulgences as chard, summer squash, radishes, snap peas and kohlrabi that had to be eaten fresh— too impractical to can.

Mother used the hot-water-bath approach to canning vegetables. She fully advised us kids to stay away from the stove during this crucial step, for fear of our being scalded by hot water or injured by an exploding jar. Jars full of product were sealed, then immersed in the water-bath canner, which was heated to boiling atop the stove. This process vacuum-sealed the jars through the dynamic of heat and pressure.

The water-bath vat accommodated eight jars at one time. During the season, Mother was at this all day long for weeks on end. A wire rack inside the kettle kept jars from knocking against each other in the boiling water. Mother heedfully lifted the hot jars to safety, making room for another round without having to let the hot water in the canning bath cool.

We planted corn on the east edge of the kitchen garden, so there we begin. Aside from drying left-over sweet corn and making Chow Chow corn relish, I do not recall if we canned our sweet corn *per se*, off the cob.

Cucumbers grew in the garden next to the corn. We reserved the bulk of the cucumbers for pickling-- roughly 80 percent of the harvest. As with the corn, we ate our fill of fresh cucumbers. We did not cook them. Isn't that odd? Some vegetables you cook and others you don't. Cucumbers are in the gourd family as are watermelons and squash-- we stored a few cucumbers in a peck basket in the fruit cellar with the other gourds.

Next in line came cabbage, which had wide uses. In the fruit cellar, alongside the cucumbers, bushel baskets of whole green cabbages sat. We didn't grow purple cabbage. Sauerkraut was an outlet for shredded cabbage. We also enjoyed cabbage raw as coleslaw— the word derives from the Dutch words for "cabbage salad." We also used up cabbage by serving it fried or boiled as a side dish on the supper table.

Moving along the rows, our garden was awash in tomatoes. Mother canned them by the boatload. We also ate sliced, fresh tomatoes at the table. We didn't grow cherry or Roma tomatoes, just the one kind, beefsteaks. Mother picked our tomatoes by the bushel. She had a practiced eye for determining ripeness. We helped her carry the bushels into the kitchen. She placed the tomatoes carefully into a sink full of cold water. She washed them and removed an occasional stem, then placed the tomatoes gently, one by one, into a pot of boiling water to blanch (*sans "e"*) them for three minutes. This prepped the skins for quick removal.

WE ALWAYS GIGGLED AT THE COOKING TERM, *BLANCH*-- MIMICKING MOTHER'S NAME SO. I'M GIGGLING NOW.

My dear mater rescued each 'mater from the boiling water with a slotted spoon and laid them in a colander. Slipping off the hot skins which separated easily, she was careful to avoid scorching her fingers. The tomatoes were ready for one-quart Mason jars, lined up on the kitchen table. Mother placed the whole tomatoes deftly into glass "lightning style" canning jars. When the jars were filled to the brim, she slowly poured in boiling water-- careful to avoid cracking the jar. Before placing the glass lids, she set a red rubber gasket atop each to ensure a seal. A lip on the gasket facilitated handling. The glass lid had a raised crown atop. A groove in the crown accommodated the wire bail for a snug seal. The bail's unique hinge design acted as a simple, barely-springy lever.

In the 40's, Mom switched to zinc screw-type caps.

After sealing the jars, she placed them onto the rack, then lowered the assemblage into the water bath. The canner itself had a sizeable metal lid and Mother placed that on the canner. Later, after the jars were sealed, she set them out to cool.

"All hands on deck"— all of us kids-- proudly carried the cooled jars down to the fruit cellar. The process of canning took most of an entire day, as only eight jars at once fit into the canner. The water-bath canning method was straightforward, safe in cautious hands and indispensable— it served for almost all our fruits and vegetables. What a workhorse.

---

*M*Y CO-AUTHOR HEARD OF A UNIVERISTY BIOLOGY LABORATORY ACCIDENT—AN AUTOCLAVE BLEW UP. AUTOCLAVES STERILIZE METAL SURGICAL INSTRUMENTS, VIA STEAM AT EXTREMELY HIGH TEMPERATURES AND PRESSURES.
A MACHINE BOLT FROM THE AUTOCLAVE WAS EXPELLED AS A RESULT OF THE EXPLOSION, WITH SUCH FORCE THAT IT TORE THROUGH THREE SUCCESSIVE WALLS IN THE BUILDING AND EMBEDDED INTO A FOURTH WALL.
THE BOLT BLEW OUT OF THERE LIKE A BOLT OUT OF THE BLUE.

IN THE 1960's, I WAS REMINDED JUST HOW SAFE BLANCHE'S WATER-BATH CANNER WAS. MY SISTER ELAINE WAS COOKING TOMATO SAUCE IN A PRESSURE COOKER THAT BLEW ITS LID LIKE MOUNT VESUVIUS. LIQUEFIED TOMATOES SPLATTERED ALL OVER HER KITCHEN-- THE FORCE OF IMPACT EMBEDDED TOMATOES INTO (NOT ONLY ONTO) THE WALLS. SHE CLEANED UP TOMATO SAUCE FOR WEEKS. WHAT A MESS!

Mother canned more than 100 quarts of tomatoes a season. A bushel of fresh tomatoes rendered down to 20 quart jars or thereabouts.

Green beans were prepared in much the same way. We children picked the mature green beans and placed them in a peck basket made of pressed, thin wood with a pressed-wood handle. Green beans were nice, fun to pick and we had lots of them—they're still my favorite vegetable. We washed the beans, broke off the ends and parboiled the beans in slightly salted water. They fit nicely into quart canning jars. We left them whole. Mother saved the water from precooking the beans to pour over the contents of the jars, then sealed them. She used the same hot-water canning method as for the tomatoes.

Mother stuck with her water-bath canner until after the War [World War II]. She acquired a pressure canner in the late 40's or early 50's. This made her canning efforts a lot easier and a *lotter* safer-- a large vat of boiling water on a stove is a fearsome thing, especially with little kids around-- lots of kids got scalded in other families.

---

EVEN TODAY, COMPANIES STAGE RECALLS FOR CANNED GREEN BEANS SUSPECTED OF CONTAMINATION. THE FDA (TECHNICALLY CREATED IN 1930) OVERSEES RECALLS. SOMETIMES, IN OUR FRUIT CELLAR, A SEAL ON ONE OF THE MASON JARS FAILED— FORCING THE LIQUID TO BUBBLE OUT. THESE BROKEN-SEALED JARS WERE TAINTED (OF COURSE) SO WE DID NOT EAT THE CONTENTS AND DIDN'T DARE FEED SUCH TO THE PIGS. CANNED GREEN BEANS ARE NOTORIOUSLY ASSOCIATED WITH BOTULISM. BUT NONE OF US EVER GOT SICK FROM ANY OF MOTHER'S CANNED FOODS. DAD WARNED US NOT TO EAT TOO MANY CUCUMBERS LEST WE CONTRACT "CHOLERY MORBUS," BUT WE WERE NOT CONCERNED WITH GETTING *KLEPTOMAINE* POISONING.

---

I have no recollection of putting up peas. I knew we grew them and had them at the table, but I don't recall canning them. I think they were too mushy to can.

Moving along through the garden in the order it was planted-- we pulled beets in late summer. If we let them grow larger than a tennis ball, they got a little woody. We sliced off root and tops. The tops went in the slop bucket under the sink. The roots were thrown away. We washed the beets thoroughly several times, then boiled them to facilitate removal of the skins. The beets were sliced and placed in quart jars.

We bought salt in 25-pound bags, stored in the landing on the steps to the second floor. Mother made a salt solution— a weak salt solution— to pour over the beets in the jar. These were lidded and put in the hot water cooker too. We ate the beets later as a garnish for the table or Mother used beets further to make her famous pickled eggs.

What more to say about the Swiss chard? We didn't put it up in jars. We had to eat it fresh.

Carrots were processed much the same as beets, except they were placed in pint, not quart jars. Mother removed the tops and root, then used a potato peeler to remove the peel.

We planted rhubarb on the extreme south edge of the garden from the center to the west corner. We called it "pie plant." Mother did just that— she made many rhubarb pies that were worth coming home from school for. We harvested rhubarb by cutting off the stalks at the base, not by pulling it up by the roots like potatoes or radishes. Harvested in this way, rhubarb came back year after year. In the house, Mother removed the green leaves, washed the stalks thoroughly in cold water and cut them into three-inch sections. She boiled the rhubarb nuggets in a sugar solution and canned the rhubarb just like the other vegetables.

*I*S RHUBARB A FRUIT OR A VEGETABLE-- WHO MAKES PIES OUT OF VEGETABLES? QUICHE IS A PIE MADE FROM EGGS AND CHEESE. SWEET POTATO PIE IS POPULAR IN THE SOUTH. RHUBARB GROWS IN THE GARDEN SO IT MUST BE A VEGETABLE. BUT I ALWAYS THOUGHT OF RHUBARB AS A FRUIT, LIKE APPLES. (WHERE COULD WE GO TO GET A PIECE OF RHUBARB PIE?)

That concludes the list of vegetables we canned from our kitchen garden. We did raise other vegetables outside the boundaries of the garden. Since pumpkins and potatoes required more space than the vegetable garden could accommodate, we planted the potatoes in their own plot to the east of and behind the house (directly across the driveway from the vegetable garden). The pumpkins grew in-between the rows of field corn, in a small area close to the north side of the house. We raised just a few pumpkins. But they were big. Big enough to make five or six pies apiece. The field corn occupied six acres of our land, extending from Route 534 to the cemetery up on Western Reserve Road.

# *P*ICKLING IN:

- **VINEGAR.**

- **BRINE (SALT WATER).**

# VINEGAR PICKLING: HOMEMADE PICKLES.

Mother preserved cucumbers by the pickling-in-vinegar method. She was famous for her pickles. She never won a ribbon in homemaking competitions at Mahoning County's annual Canfield Fair. Then again, she never entered any contests. Her bread-and-butter pickles, sweet gherkins and whole dill pickles were prizes on our table.

'Round about June, Mother selected thumb-sized cukes from the garden for her pickling enterprise. These fledglings made gherkins. Contrary to myth, pickling does not shrink cucumbers any more than boiling an egg shrinks the egg. To make itty-bitty pickles like gherkins, start with itty-bitty cucumbers. Pickling marinade was made of water, vinegar, salt, a pinch of alum to impart crispness, and sweetened with a little saccharine—cheaper and sweeter than sugar, it stretched further. (We watched pennies during the Depression.)

Ho-Ho-Ho and Merry Crispness!

The Watkins Spice man provided all our spices. We put the cucumbers up in pint jars. I do not recall having to cook the jars in the hot-water canner. I think Mother put the pickles up cold. Vinegar took care of any *contaminincantations*.

Of the remaining cucumbers, Mother let some remain on the vine until they grew to about five inches in length. These she selected for dill pickles and for bread-and-butter pickles.

Mother grew dill in her garden. She used dill seeds to flavor the brine to create dill pickles. As an added flourish, she placed a feathery sprig of dill on top of the pickles before she put the lid on.

The pickles were ready after about a month of soaking in the vinegar solution.

Mother spiced her bread-and-butter pickles with turmeric powder and mustard seed. For these pickles, she cut cucumbers into half-inch slices, sweetened with saccharin also. She placed the slices in a pan and poured in the pickling marinade. She loaded the jars right out of the pan. A handful of slices filled up a pint jar.

The remaining cukes were allowed to mature on the vine to seven or eight inches in length. They got real bitter if they were allowed to grow longer than that. These were too big for pickling and were destined instead for the table to be eaten fresh (sliced and served plain) or with Mother's dressing-- soured cream made from fresh cream and a splash of vinegar.

## Vinegar Pickling: Chow Chow Relish.

Making Chow Chow relish was quite simple. Mom selected virgin ears of sweet corn, fresh from the garden.

The ears were shucked, boiled, then laid out to cool completely. She used a paring knife to cut the kernels from the cobs. Dad kept Mother's paring knives honed to a sharp edge-- many a cut finger ensued from these razor-edged knives.

The kernels were placed in a large bowl and conjoined with diced fresh onions (Mother's standby ingredient). Over this combination she poured a cold, dilute solution of vinegar sweetened with saccharine. She then filled pint jars with this mixture and screwed the lids down tight. The jars of relish were stored in the fruit cellar. As I said, this was a simple process.

SOUTH ON ROUTE 534, JUST OVER STRATTON'S HILL, LIVED A LADY NAMED HATTIE WESTON. SHE WAS AN OLD SPINSTER WHO HAD A GARDEN. WHEN ELAINE AND I WALKED TO SCHOOL, HATTIE APPROACHED THE EDGE OF HER DRIVEWAY. "HOW DOES YOUR MAMMA MAKE CHOW CHOW?" SHE ASKED US. WE LOOKED AT EACH OTHER AND SHRUGGED OUR SHOULDERS. WE DIDN'T KNOW! SHE DIDN'T ASK US JUST ONCE. SHE ASKED US MANY TIMES. WE KIDS NEVER TOOK TIME TO ASK MOTHER FOR THE RECIPE. "HOW DOES YOUR MAMMA MAKE CHOW CHOW?" BECAME A STANDING JOKE IN OUR FAMILY. WHEN SOMEONE WANTED TO MAKE THE OTHERS LAUGH, THEY POSED THIS QUESTION. IT INVARIABLY INVOKED GIGGLES.

Chow Chow was originally popular in Pennsylvania and in the South. It can be made from any locally-available vegetables.  If we had red or green sweet bell peppers (which we didn't), Mother would've added some of those too for show, finely minced.

The origin of the term, "Chow Chow" is of uncertain etymology, including one unsavory idea connecting Chinese food with a dog breed, the Chow Chow.  Another theory posits that the name is based on the French word for "cabbage," *chou*.  Chou Chou?  Choo Choo?

Various meat dishes were complimented by the Chow Chow relish.  A little bit of it went a long way.

## PICKLING IN BRINE:  SAUERKRAUT.

We made sauerkraut by the pickling-in-brine method (by contrast, we made pickles by the pickling-in-vinegar method).  We used a cabbage slicer/shredder of simple construction-- a metal blade imbedded at an angle in a flat wooden housing about 6 inches wide by 18 inches long. Wooden rails on each side kept the cabbage on track.  We used this kitchen gadget to shred the cabbage into thin strips. We kids asked Mother for the heart of the cabbage when she was done shredding.  The heart was good eaten raw with salt on it, a true treat in the days before snack food—to this day still a treat.

We employed 20-gallon crocks to make sauerkraut. We placed a five-inch layer of the prepared cabbage into the bottom of the crock.  We then dusted that layer with a handful of salt. More layers of shredded cabbage and salt followed until the cabbage was about an inch or so from the brim. We did not need to add water to the crock, only salt. The action of the dry salt upon the dry, cut cabbage drew water out of the cabbage, which is about 70 percent water. Even with that inch of head room, sometimes the crock still overflowed during the fermentation process. We set a large dinner plate on top of the final stratum of cabbage (not on top of the crock proper). We then situated a special, large stone atop this plate. The weight of the stone helped the plate to settle in, to press into solution the water drawn out of the cabbage. The plate also helped keep the juices in the crock— except when it overflowed.

After about four to six weeks, our family enjoyed freshly made sauerkraut at the table, most often with a main meat dish of pork chops or sausage.

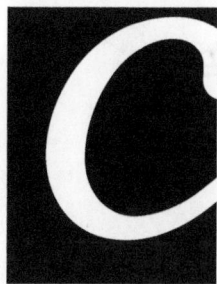

## COOL STORAGE.

Cool-storing vegetables (and fruits) in the basement without precooking, pickling or canning was another tool available to us for preserving food. We stored apples, beets, heads of cabbages, kohlrabi, onions, potatoes, pumpkins and acorn squash by this means.

# fRUIT Conservation.

The only cultivable fruit we grew within the confines of our farm were elderberries, gooseberries and plums. I include rhubarb here because I still think of it as a fruit. We did have several apple trees, but the fruit on them was so gnarly and insect-bitten they could not be described as either edible or cannable—bugs had already *can-nibble-ized* them.

## fRUIT WE GREW FOR CANNING.

- ELDERBERRIES.
- GOOSEBERRIES.
- PLUMS.
- RHUBARB. (CORRECT, A VEGETABLE.)

## fRUIT FREELY BESTOWED OR FINAGLED.

- BLACKBERRIES.
- CONCORD GRAPES.

## fRESH FRUIT WE BOUGHT FOR CANNING.

- APPLES.
- CHERRIES.
- PEACHES.
- STRAWBERRIES.

In addition to Mother's considerable endeavor to can hundreds of jars of tomatoes and other vegetables, she stored fruit that was otherwise perishable. Our family ate fruits conserved two ways: as bread spreads or as pie fillings/table condiments. First were the jellies, jams, preserves and spreads she put up. Mother made these gems— I mean *jams*— with peaches, berries and other fruits. (We had access to neither apricots nor raspberries.) The preserves tasted so good on Mother's home made bread and butter. Second, came pie fillings she canned, which doubled as side dishes when not put into pie crusts-- a dish of canned peaches, say.

# f RUIT SMEAR-ONS.

Fruits Mother put up in jam jars for use on bread included:

---

### GENERIC CATEGORY: BREAD SMEAR-ONS

**J**ELLIES: ELDERBERRY, GRAPE

**J**AMS: GOOSEBERRY, BLACKBERRY, STRAWBERRY

**P**RESERVES: USING QUARTERED OR HALF CHUNKS OF WHOLE FRUIT: PEACH, PLUM

**S**PREADS: APPLE SAUCE, APPLE BUTTER

---

We only pilfered one fruit: blackberries. We didn't really pilfer them. Mother, at some point in time, had received permission from our neighbor, Mr. Oliver Smith, to pick all the berries we wanted, at will, from his side of the fence. There was nobody else to pick them.

"Smithy," as we called him, was a hermit. He stayed indoors mostly-- not outdoors much, picking berries or anything else, that we could tell. His place, 100 acres or more, was covered with woods and briers. His property adjoined Willow Run along our eastern boundary. His spread *spread* from Western Reserve Road (to the north) and to VonKaenel's farm (to the south).

No one lived across Seacrist Road at that time. And even though he was our neighbor, Smithy's small house was way over on Seacrist Road— a mile from our home. VonKaenel's house faced Calla Road. These factors— along with the size of his property, only increased Smithy's apparent isolation.

There were no domesticated animals on Smithy's holdings. I don't know if he had a dog or a cat or a raven or a tame squirrel as a companion. There were no cultivated crops over there. Just snaggled-over woods and briers. Nothing.

Kind of spooky.

Mother cautioned us kids never to go near his place. Oliver Smith lived alone. How he ate, fed himself, how he washed his clothes (if at all) or how he survived--

we never knew.  Did anyone visit him?  Who knows?  I have not the slightest idea where he got food or potable water.  Did he have a sister or brother or kindly-or-otherwise nephew who brought in supplies and a hot meal for him from time to time?  We never knew.

I never learned what became of Mr. Smith or his woods or his 100-plus acres.  Or if he had a family or if anyone came to see him.  It's a big mystery.

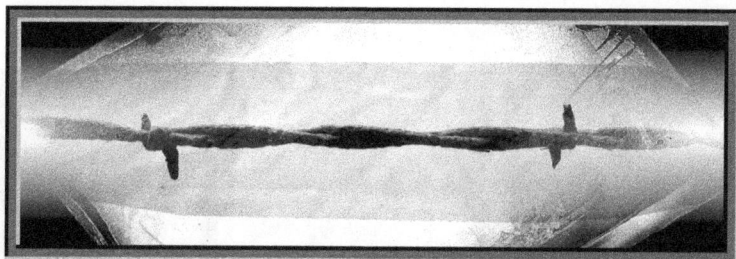

# fRUIT WE CANNED FOR PIES & SIDE DISHES AT THE TABLE.

A list of fruit that Mother canned in quart jars for later use in double-crust pies or for table use as side dishes or desserts includes:

# *THE FRUIT CELLAR:*
# *THE WOOLF'S "CANNERY ROW."*

Back to the basement. After the quarts, pints and jelly jars of produce were sealed and cooled, we kids proudly carried them to the fruit cellar to align on the shelves. They were not lined up willy-nilly but arranged by category. They were! They were like soldiers bedecked in their finery for a colorful parade. Red tomatoes, yellow cherries, blue plums, blackberries and every hue in the rainbow in-between.

In the southwest corner of the basement was our prize plum-- the fruit cellar. It was quite extensive. The shelving system Dad built stood about six foot high. He crafted the first shelf ankle height off the floor. These shelves lined the three walls on the west half of the cellar (extending from about a third of the south wall, running along most of the west wall, and the portion of the north wall enclosing the furnace). Dad made the shelves nice and deep. They could accommodate 300 to 400 jars. With Mother putting up 50 quarts of peaches or 100 jars of tomatoes at a crack (without breaking a single jar) the shelves were laden full by the close of canning season. To Dad's credit, the shelving was practical. To Mother's credit, these shelves were filled with row upon row of glass jars full of jeweled delicacies for the colorless months ahead.

Our very own grocery store.

In the center of the fruit cellar, big white onions hung from the beams. We stored white potatoes in burlap bags that simply sat on the cool dirt floor. The whole idea of the fruit cellar: temperate enough both summer and winter to conserve but not roast or freeze the goods. Mother, a good quartermaster, ensured that the root vegetables, bulbs and tubers in storage had been consumed well before the thick of summer rolled in.

We stored beets and cabbages in wooden fruit crates on the floor. We stored pumpkins and other squash on the floor, as these didn't need to be in crates. The acorn and summer squash we grew was eaten fresh only. We consumed pumpkins at a faster rate because they spoiled more quickly than, say, potatoes. Mother used our pumpkins for pie, especially at Thanksgiving.

In wooden boxes next to the potatoes sat apples, beets, chard, leftover cabbages, carrots and kohlrabies. We were obliged to consume the fresh-picked chard within a week or so of harvest, as noted.

Sauerkraut percolated in a pair of 20-gallon crocks that sat near Mother's egg-candling workbench.

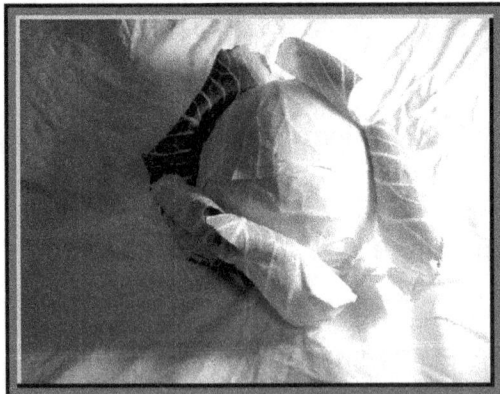

Mother had her hands full during the year: putting in the garden during spring, putting up tomato stakes in the garden during the summer, putting up preserves during the fall, putting up her feet during the winter to produce a quilt, and putting up with Dad and us kids around the clock. In addition to these assembly-line duties related to raising our own food, Mother had additional tasks, upon which I now reflect.

---

ONE OF DAD'S MANY WITS:
"WE EAT WHAT WE CAN AND WHAT WE CAN'T EAT WE CAN."

# VIGNETTE: PUNCHY FRIENDS.

IN THE 1980'S, A GOLF FRIEND ROUTINELY DROPPED THREE OR FOUR HOMEGROWN, MEGA-TON ZUCCHINI ON ME EVERY WEEK DURING GOLF SEASON, YEAR UPON YEAR. SHE BROUGHT SACKS FULL OF THESE SQUASH TO DUMP ON ALL COMRADES IN OUR LADIES' LEAGUE. EACH WEIGHED AT LEAST 20 POUNDS (EACH SQUASH, THAT IS, NOT EACH COMRADE).

HOWEVER, INVARIABLY, AS SOON AS I PULLED OUT OF THE PARKING LOT AND WAS OUTSIDE EYE-SHOT OF THE CLUBHOUSE, I ROLLED DOWN MY WINDOW AND TOSSED THE LOT OUT.

ALL THE WHILE, I HOPED THE DONOR WAS NOT FOLLOWING BEHIND IN HER CAR. SHE WOULD HAVE RUN OVER THE GIANTS, SQUASHING HER OWN SQUASH ON THE ROADWAY. AND ME? I WOULD HAVE BEEN IN A STEW TO EXPLAIN MY CHEEKY SELF.

# CHAPTER 16:
## MOTHER & HER OTHER INDUSTRIES.

**DAFFYNITION.** *PULLET'S-UR-PRIZE: AWARDED WHEN A CHICKEN LAYS A DOUBLE-YOLKED, BLUE-RIBBON EGG.*

1934 is as good a year as any to take a snapshot of my mother and her household duties apart from handling food. She was 40 that year. My little brother, Homer, was 8 and I was 10. He was the baby of the family and he was still being babied.

Even after 24 years of married life, Mother still reserved a warm smile for a tramp begging a cold lunch on a hot day. Even in middle age, Mother had not become embittered by years of endless, thankless domestic duty on a working farm. She had become slightly stout. She had borne six children.

This particular morning, her thick, chestnut-brown hair was put up in a bun, as usual when she was working. Her homemade apron was not made from the ubiquitous sugar sacks. Timeworn but clean, it boasted a whimsical floral pattern in bright reds, yellows and blues. The multicolored fabric was one of the few whimsies in which she indulged.

"Mom! The Watkins man is here!" Homer and I said, in unison. We catapulted into the kitchen.

"Don't SLA-am the screen door!" Mother said, her one-millionth admonishment. The screen door slammed behind us anyway. With five of us yet at home, Mother still had a twinkle in her light-blue eyes, even when scolding us. We dance-hopped around her as she wiped her hands on the sides of her apron. She untied her apron and lifted it over her head-- threw it over a kitchen chair. No time for hanging it on a nail in the cellarway. She patted down her wavy hair as she headed out the screen door, pausing to close it gently. She came off the back porch with a quick step and greeted the spice salesman. She was thrilled at the prospect of sharing pleasantries for a few, savory moments with an adult.

A flour-dust fingerprint was on her left cheek-- evidence of her early-morning bread baking...

The Watkins man came by only once a year. Mother was smiling broadly by now. She could replenish her cupboard with the spices that added an irresistible touch to her home-baked pies, custards and puddings. Her bread pudding was good! As the Watkins man opened the door of his black Model A sedan, Mother caught the slightest sense of exotic scents and adventures captured from distant lands. The slight, sweet aromas—imagined, perhaps-- of cinnamon, allspice, ginger, nutmeg and cloves hung in the air. For an instant, she was thinking about foreign lands and far-off things, not Berlin Center, Ohio, at all.

# CLOTHES TENDING.

## MONDAY: WASHDAY.

Monday was always washday at our house. A washtub stood in the northeast corner of the cellar. Dad installed hooks in the joists supporting the kitchen floor. From the hooks, he suspended clotheslines running north to south in the basement. Fall and winter, Mother hung clean, wet clothes on these lines. The sun in those seasons was insufficient to dry laundry outdoors. Heavy snowfalls and thermometers showing just a hint of red added to the impracticality of hanging clothes outside during cold months. We kids had fun ducking in and out of the hanging clothes and bed sheets, playing tag or pretending we were Hansel and Gretel in a forest, leaving a trail of breadcrumbs here and there. We played like that in Dad's room too (or outside in clement weather) when clothes were hanging in (or out) there to dry.

"Don't dirty the sheets," Mom said often enough while we played.

The soiled-clothes load was expansive: sheets and pillowcases from four beds; overalls, shirts, socks, stockings, underwear, dresses, table cloths, aprons.

Mother had to do laundry every Monday to keep ahead of this tremendous task.

> *I* DO NOT RECALL A WRINGER WASHER BUT SURELY MY DAD PROVIDED ONE FOR MOTHER. MY SISTER ELAINE RECALLS A HAND-CRANKED WRINGER IN THE CELLAR, CLAMPED TO THE BACK OF THE WASHTUB. ELAINE REMEMBERS THIS APPLIANCE. AS SHE TELLS IT: "I KNOW THERE WAS A WRINGER. I GOT MY HAND CAUGHT IN IT ONCE."

I must issue a *caveat* here: I find myself at a loss to explain how hot water was generated in our house.

In the 30's, manufacturers of coal furnaces offered optional-purchase attachments for hot water heaters. Domestic water heaters were available by the late 1800's. As ingenious as Dad was, and given that our basement had 1) a furnace and 2) a water well (as opposed to an oil well—can't you just see oil gushing out the chimney?), he could have devised a means to combine this <u>heat</u> and <u>water</u> to make <u>hot water</u>, and somehow pump it via pipes up to the first-floor kitchen and bathroom.

Whether Sumner Stanley purchased the furnace originally with a hot water tank or if Dad added one later (if at all) is conjecture. Clearly we never fired up the furnace in summer to wash dishes, launder clothes and bathe in hot water. Had we a water boiler attached to the furnace, Dad still would have needed a backup water-heating system for use during warm weather.

The most plausible solution to this mystery is to surmise that our house had an electric water heater. My dad ran electricity to the house in 1931 when the lines came down past the house from the town of Berlin Center. And yet I am certain we had hot water in the kitchen and bathroom sinks and in the tub before 1931. (When Mother had her "female-trouble" operation around 1929, her sister, LeeEtta, came over to help out. One Saturday evening, while Mother was recuperating upstairs, Aunt LeeEtta put Homer and me (together) in the tub and scrubbed us good, then put us to bed. And that bathwater was <u>hot</u>.)

There was no water upstairs, just our one bathroom downstairs. Anyone I could ask about this is dead, except for my sister. I did ask Elaine. You would think between the two of us— both having been born in that house— that we could remember a hot water arrangement.

By 1921, Dad had *confabricated* a rig consisting of a gasoline-engine generator, to convert gasoline fuel to electricity. The generator was hooked up to a battery that stored the freshly minted electricity for immediate or later use. Then in 1924, Dad shrewdly upgraded to a Delco system he purchased from Berlin School (perhaps at auction-- the school was placed on the grid sometime after electric lines reached Berlin Center proper in 1924, thus obviating the school's need for a generator).

I do recall Mother boiling water in a tea kettle on the stove for the express purpose of pouring hot water into the dishpan at the sink. The stove was already fired up -- she saved water by using the kettle (by not having to waste water at the spicket while waiting for the water to run hot there). Was Mother simply practicing a habit cultivated before Dad rigged up his gasoline generator prior to 1921? (Now I am further perplexed regarding how my family generated electricity—or hot water—before 1921. My parents moved to the big house in 1917. Other than boiling a pot of water on the stove-- were they without hot water there for four years?)

ELECTRIC LINES CAME PAST OUR HOUSE IN 1931 AS PART OF THE ELECTRIFICATION OF RURAL AMERICA PROGRAM (FORMALIZED BY THE CONGRESSIONAL RURAL ELECTRIFICATION ACT OF 1936 UNDER FRANKLIN ROOSEVELT). WHY IN BLAZES DID OUR TOWN FATHERS KEEP US IN THE DARK FOR SEVEN YEARS? THE ANSWER MAY LIE IN DISTRIBUTION AVENUES USED THEN— VOLTAGES DROPPED TO UNUSABLE LEVELS ON LINES CARRIED THREE OR FOUR MILES PAST MUNICIPAL POWER STATIONS. BERLIN CENTER HAD TO WAIT ON TECHNOLOGY! WHAT A *DILEM-MINNA*! THEY FIXED UP THE TOWNSFOLK IN 1924, THEN SAT AROUND UNTIL '31 SCRATCHING THEIR COLLECTIVE HEADS ABOUT HOW TO SERVICE US *RURALIES*—NOT EXACTLY LIGHTNING SPEED. THUS, IN 1931, DAD WAS ABLE TO WEAN THE WATER HEATER OFF THE GENERATOR BY WIRING THE WATER HEATER OFF THE HOUSE LINE. IS IT MERE COINCIDENCE THAT MY PARENTS STARTED THE POULTRY FARM IN (OR AROUND) 1931?

The stumper regarding our hot water system is as much an enigma as to how Oliver Smith survived as a hermit on his uncultivated land during the Depression.

Doing laundry for a family of eight was daunting. Mother had only a scrub board and the hand-cranked wringer to ease her load. A capacious laundry basket was always stationed near the chimney at the terminus of the clothes chute down cellar. Two, three or four basketsful accumulated before Mother was ready to tackle the laundry of any given Monday.

She probably piled the bulkier items on the concrete collar of the water well. Of course we kept the well covered-- we couldn't afford little kids falling into it. Mother sorted the laundry into separate piles for light and dark clothes. Another pile was reserved for sheets only.

Mother added Oxydol soap powder to the washtub filled with water. She scrubbed all the linens and clothing piece by piece on the washboard—quite unlike the modern convenience of batch-washing a load of clothes.

Using the scrub board was hard on the knuckles and hard on the back, adding to the discomfort of hands chapped and fingernails split from hand-washing heaps of dirty clothing. The water drawn from our well came up with a high mineral content. We added a teaspoon of caustic lye to the basin when washing dishes. Perhaps

Mother added lye to the washtub water as well, adding to the assault on her hands.

Florence or Doris helped Mother on washday during the summer. Mother fed the clothes into the wringer as one of my sisters cranked the handle.

The wringer was— I can't say a dangerous weapon— but it was an invention to be feared. When used with caution, it wrung excess water from clothes for quicker drying, easing Mother's burden. Used as a toy, it bit back. The wringer was always on the alert for sweet morsels-- tiny fingers, hands, strands of hair, a loose fold of clothing— to draw into its enticing maw. We small children were not allowed anywhere near the wringer, especially when Mother was wringing clothes.

After scrubbing and wringing out the laundry, Mother hung the clothes to dry. Winter created a convenience for a captive audience-- the clothes lines were a clothespin's length away from the washtub and the furnace kept the cellar cozily warm.

Regarding the clothes lines: those in the basement remained in place year 'round. The lines in Dad's room and outdoors— Dad hung up every Monday for Mother's washday, as needed. We took down the lines outdoors and in the office after each wash; otherwise, a nuisance— obstructions (hazards, really) to duck under constantly.

Hanging the wash out in summer was a chore of its own. It fell to Mother to carry the heavy basketloads of damp clothes up from the basement to the backyard. This insult only added to the injury of scrubbing the laundry by hand on a rough washboard in lye-water.

What back-breaking effort.

Dad strung the lines in the back yard from every available tree using hooks. He had forged clothes poles from pronged tree limbs to prop up sagging clotheslines. This stout **Y** kept the heavy, wet wash off the ground.

Mother wore a homemade clothespin bag around her waist. Long strings hung down in the back and the bag hung down to Mother's upper thigh. She carefully pinned clothes and sheets to the line with wooden, one-piece ("Shaker-style") pronged pegs. Atop, the pins sported a round knob for ease of handling. (Spring-loaded, two-piece pins, invented in the 1850's, allowed more give-and-take. Yet, as we have seen with many innovations from the 19th and early 20th centuries, improved clothespins had not wended their way to Willow Run Farm by the 30's.)

Every few years Mother had to make herself a new clothespin bag when the old one wore out. The bag was probably made from a sugar sack (if Mother had any fabric left over from making our knickers). Bulky affairs, these homespun bags consisted simply of one large, open compartment filled with three or four dozen pins. Mother could just reach her hand in there and grab two or three clothespins at a clip.

Summers were warm and windy enough for drying clothes outdoors. In winter or on rainy days, of course, we had to dodge clothes hanging in the cellar and in the office. In any weather—cold, wet, warm, dry (whether or not we kids were home from school to lend a hand or to agitate Mother) -- doing laundry was yet a disheartening task. Who rightly wrings their hands over having to toss a load of clothes into a modern agitator-style washer?

Summertime was ideal for laundering clothes. Drying them outdoors in a brisk breeze left them fragrantly fresh and sweet. Sometimes a summer storm rumbled up. Mother, with our help, hurriedly yanked the clothes off the line. That happened a lot. During a sudden downpour, we tried to get the clothes and ourselves back into the house without getting either drenched. It was unnerving to take down still-wet clothes outside and have to turn right around and re-hang them inside. Anyone who has ever hung heavy, soaking-wet sheets would understand.

# *t*UESDAY: IRONING DAY.

Ironing Day was Tuesday. This domestic duty Mother approached with pride. I think she kind of liked to iron. Perhaps it ironed out her nerves and surely was flat-out easier than washing clothes. Aside from having to stand on her feet, ironing gave her time to think-- about what to fix for supper or what kind of pies to bake.

Mother's electric Sunbeam was the latest wrinkle in household appliances, an improvement over gasoline-, carbide-gas- (acetylene-), natural-gas-, and kerosene-heated irons. (Irons heated by liquid fuel were sold in rural America through World War 2, despite the grotesque fire hazard.) Her electric model allowed her ironing to go smoothlier. The ironing board folded down neatly from its upright position in the cupboard, to the left of the screen door-- really a work of art.

Mother had to dampen the clothes beforehand, as the Sunbeam was not a steam iron. On Monday nights, she worked at the kitchen table. She dipped her hand into a bowl of warm water and used an underhand stroke to sprinkle the fabric— skirts, dresses, blouses, pillowcases, shirts. She rolled each article tight to keep the item damp overnight. The rolls she stacked sideways into a wicker basket to await the morning.

Tuesday morning, after breakfast was finished and the table cleared, Mother began her ironing. Mother folded and placed each freshly ironed piece of clothing onto a pile segregated for each child. She stacked the piles into clothesbaskets.

Overalls, socks, towels, underwear and sheets went un-ironed.

Mother set the baskets heaped with folded clothes near the door to the second floor. An unwritten house rule stipulated that the next able-bodied person going upstairs took along anything staged there, in this instance a basket of ironed clothes. This arrangement, a real time-and-effort saver, was the bucket brigade in reverse, wherein the last one down had to carry the bucket outdoors.

With the ironing done, Mother left the ironing board down until the Sunbeam cooled, which didn't take long. When not in use, the iron tucked into a little nook in the bottom of the cupboard. Then Mother put them all up—the ironing board, the iron and her feet.

## GG HANDLING.

Egg handling was another responsibility that fell to Mother. Among all Mother's varied occupations on our farm, I think she was proud of this one above all others. She took pride in her ability to sort eggs on a small scale and to contribute to the household income on a larger scale.

We raised chickens. My father had built a structure measuring 40 by 80 foot, at the top of the barn hill in

1930 or 1931 (before that, he worked on the Pennsylvania Railroad as a carpenter). This building was always known as the "laying house." It held 500 adult chickens raised from our own baby chicks. On the north wall was the roosting area and on the west wall four tiers of nests. The hens laid their eggs in these nests. It was up to us kids to gather the eggs. Twice daily, we carried a wire egg basket up to the laying house for this chore. When an egg basket was full (with about 100 eggs), two of us carried it down the hill and into the basement. We did not cushion the eggs while they lay stacked in the basket. We simply laid them in gingerly. (Lo and behold if we stumbled while hurrying down the hill!) Mother's pride in her egg handling was based in part on the fact that she did it so well. This was, yet, a chore.

But Mother, by her good nature, had a tendency to let herself see the best in everybody and in everything. So, true to her nature, sorting eggs became a way for her to sit for a while

and sort out her thoughts. She sat on a tall stool in the cellar, at the table Dad had built for her. This space underneath the window in the south wall of the cellar was Mom's office.

Perhaps she hummed to herself as she went through the eggs by the dozens. Perhaps earlier in the day, she had begun to make bread. She had a large, metal pan accommodating dough for six loaves of bread at a punch. Fall through early spring, Mother set this pan on the register in the living room to kick-start the yeast to rising. As she settled in to handle the eggs, she could have been musing about finishing her bread baking or wondering if she needed to iron her white dress for an upcoming Pythian Sisters meeting Thursday evening.

Once she set to it, finishing the task begun by the laying hens went fast. Bits of straw, chicken dung and dried egg yolk had to be removed from soiled shells before the eggs could be sold or consumed.

She sorted the eggs into four categories. Priority fell to eggs destined for a coop— oops! That should be spelled, "co-op." Working throughout the week, Mother settled these eggs into wooden crates provided by the Columbiana County Egg Cooperative. The Co-op driver picked up these cartons every Thursday around noon. The Co-op bookkeeper sent Dad a check a week later for the eggs we shipped. That household income went not to Mother directly but mostly to Hawkins Mill (to buy more chicken feed).

The Co-Op gave us 50 cents per dozen eggs. These first-tier eggs were *la crème de la crème* of the crop. The Co-op expected that Mother send only the best. By her own integrity, she ensured that every egg for the Co-op crate was unblemished. This meant perfect shells: no cracks, no debris, clean Clean CLEAN. (Today, free-range chicken eggs at the Farmers Market sell for $3.75/dozen.)

Dad or Delmus hefted the loaded egg crates upstairs. In summer, he set them on the back porch to await the Co-op man. In winter, we left the crates in the kitchen.

**FARM FRESH EGGS**

Figure 3: TYPICAL WOODEN EGG CRATE. ILLUSTRATION BY M. GRENGA.

The Egg Co-op op-erated out of Columbiana. They sold my mother's eggs to commercial kitchens, restaurants, hotels, grocery stores— the local A&P grocery store, who knows?

The second tier consisted of slightly cracked eggs, perfectly useable. Mother sold these to our neighbors at the embarrassingly-low price of 25 cents per dozen.

Local farm wives and other neighbors came by to pick up their eggs, to chat and to gossip. It was a good excuse for a neighbor lady (who didn't raise her own hens) to walk down to our place for a visit with Mother. A tall man came by Sunday evenings, always while we were eating supper. I never knew his name or where he lived. We always called him "Tall Man."

Kitchen eggs made up the third category-- those not sold to the Co-op or neighbors. Kitchen eggs were marred a bit— a chip here or a crushed spot there. Mother did not sell all the eggs our farm produced—she needed a substantial quantity for our kitchen. Thus she reserved for our household use the most blemished.

My dad allowed Mother to keep her income from egg sales to the neighbors. She kept her egg money in a jelly jar on a shelf in the kitchen. Quarters, dimes and nickels accumulated week by week. Mother reserved these coins for indulgences— dues for the Pythian Sisters, sundries from the grocery truck, a favored Love Nest candy bar ( a nut roll—chocolate-covered peanuts and caramel over a fudge center, akin to Baby Ruth, Oh Henry!, Old Nick and Chicken Dinner bars), or socks and gloves for us kids. (Years later, she used her Social Security check to buy socks and gloves for her grandchildren.)

The fourth and final egg-handling category involved candling every egg with a light bulb to cull out fertile eggs. These were headed for *inky-bators* my dad purchased in 1934 as a money-saving and money-making strategy. This lucky strike turned out to be a geyser-- into the 1940's we sold baby chicks and "started pullets" to local dairy farmers at a modest but viable profit.

# COAL MAN.

Mother knew when to expect the coal delivery man. We placed orders a day or two ahead. He showed up at the back door.

"Wouldja open the cellar window, Ma'am?"

The coal man did not have a dump truck, just a flatbed truck with built-up sides. He came up the drive and drove across the lawn where he backed up to the northwest corner of the house. The window there allowed him to shovel coal directly onto the basement floor in the coal bin. With a wide shovel, he transferred the dusty black load into the coal room via a portable wooden chute he carried on the truck. He probably brought about half a ton of coal each time, which had to be unloaded by hand. The coal man was adept at this heavy labor.

We kids and Dad could always tell when the coal man had come, because his truck left tire marks on the lawn.

When finished, the coal man went around to the back door again. Mother paid him with cash. We had no checkbook. I imagine a load of coal was two dollars. The coal man's face and hands were streaked with sweat and soot. He did not come into the house to wash up. Mother paid him and he was on his way. They didn't stretch out this transaction. He washed up at the outdoor spicket and left.

## *t*HE ICE MAN CAMETH.

In summer, the ice man came on Saturdays. In those days, we didn't call the vehicles "pick-ups," they were "trucks." The ice man arrived in an old truck. He parked just off the road by the front yard. He didn't drive into the driveway. We kids rushed out to greet him, begging for chips of ice. He graciously gave us small slivers that had chipped off the blocks. What a treat in a freezerless household. He knew Mother needed a single block each week. He picked the block up with ice tongs, slung it over his back and delivered it into the kitchen— dripping all the way like a one-horse open sleigh.

It was always nice to have a fresh block in the ice box, just like it was always comforting to have a topped-off pile of coal in the basement. But that was summer and winter— the iceman stood down in winter and the coal man stood down in summer. (Makes me wonder what the coal man did in summer for income and vice-virtue for the ice man in winter.)

A block of ice cost 50 cents, delivered. Mother had to sell the equivalent of two dozen cracked eggs to pay for one block of ice.

It was like one big bartering bazaar.

The ice kept our milk and cream cool and that was well worth a half-dollar.

Once Mother paid the ice man, he had to make haste to his other customers before his wares melted. He kept the ice covered with heavy tarpaulins to keep the sun at bay. The bed of his truck was open and flat, no roof, no covering, just the tarp and slat sides to protect the ice from disappearing or sliding off the truck-- the last lady on his route merited getting her money's worth.

## WATKINS SPICE MAN.

"Mom! The Watkins man's here!" we kids yelled as we ran into the kitchen, letting the screen door bang loudly. We didn't wait for Mother to tidy up. The door slammed behind us again as we tore back outside.

The Watkins man pulled his Model A car into the driveway. The driver's side door sported a sign that read:

# WATKINS SPICES

Mother was elated he'd arrived, at last. He only visited once a year, in the summer. Mother was prepared for him. We didn't make grocery lists. Mother had a mental list of exactly what she needed. A typical spice list:

- ALLSPICE
- ALUM
- BAKING POWDER
- CINNAMON, GROUND OR IN STICKS
- CLOVES, WHOLE
- GINGER, GROUND
- MUSTARD, GROUND OR SEEDS
- NUTMEG, GROUND
- PECTIN
- PEPPER, BLACK, GROUND
- TURMERIC
- VANILLA, LIQUID

Mother knew exactly how long a can of ground mustard, for instance, lasted our family of eight. She knew exactly what she wanted to purchase. She was also relieved for the opportunity to get out of the kitchen for a few minutes to exchange pleasantries with someone. Anyone provided a welcome respite from us kids slamming the screen door all the time and playing tag in the house.

Mother paid and thanked him. He was on his way-- lots of farms to service. He came out of Alliance, went as far west as Deerfield, Ohio—a large enough territory.

Now I'm in a bind, I have no idea how much Mom paid for a year's worth of baking supplies. Watkins's colorful tins made a lively display in the kitchen cupboard. The tins had those strange little lids imbedded in the top which had to be pried open. The mustard came in yellow cans. Some spices came in little red cans.

These neighbors and vendors were the regular commercial visitors with whom Mother interacted during her workday: the egg Co-op man, neighbors looking to buy eggs, the coal man, ice man and Watkins Spice man.

*Mother raised six healthy children. She wished only the best for my father and us kids. Her death in 1966 ended my parents' 56-year marriage. I think of her juggling clothespins while trying to hang wet, cold bed sheets in a whipping wind; being spattered on her hands with sizzling hot bacon grease at our coal-fired stove; peeling hundreds of bushels of potatoes; baking how many thousands of pies; lovingly washing our clothes by hand. Mother was remarkable. Through the hard years of the Depression, she never became a hard person. The inauspicious beginning of her forced marriage at age 15 to my father did not daunt her spirit. Like the person she was, she carried grace and kindness into it and made the best of all of it. I am a better person for having known her.*

# Vignette: Lye Punch.

*a*FTER SUPPER, MOTHER AND DAD HAD GONE UPSTAIRS TO CHANGE INTO THEIR LODGE CLOTHES. MOTHER SERVED SUPPER EVERY NIGHT PROMPTLY AT 6. LODGE WAS EVERY THURSDAY EVENING AT 7, SO SOME BUSTLE WAS GOING ON. DORIS AND ELAINE WERE RESPONSIBLE FOR DOING THE DISHES THAT NIGHT. THEY WERE STILL CLEARING THE TABLE AS MY FOLKS HEADED OUT THE BACK DOOR. MEANWHILE, I WAS MOST LIKELY CHASING HOMER AROUND THE LIVING ROOM.

"DON'T SLAM THE SCREEN DOOR!" ELAINE SAID TO MY FOLKS. MOTHER CHUCKLED AT THIS SMART-ALECKYISM.

A TEASPOON OF LYE DUMPED INTO THE DISH PAN SOFTENED THE HARD WATER FROM OUR WELL. ON THIS OCCASION, DORIS DUMPED LYE INTO THE DISHPAN AND UNTHINKINGLY LAID THE SPOON ONTO A PLATE THAT REMAINED ON THE TABLE-- THE KITCHEN TABLE WAS CLOSE TO THE SINK. A DUSTING OF LYE COATED THE SPOON. I SAUNTERED IN, OUT OF BREATH, AND ESPIED THE SPOON. TO ME IT LOOKED INVITINGLY LIKE WHITE SUGAR. I UNTHINKINGLY PICKED UP THE SPOON, LICKED IT AND QUICKLY REALIZED IT WAS NOT SWEET. MY TONGUE BURNED HORRIBLY. BY THEN, I KNEW TO AVOID SWALLOWING WHATEVER IT WAS—SPARING MY THROAT WHILE MY TONGUE BLAZED. DODIE REALIZED I HAD LICKED THE LYE OFF THAT SPOON. THANKFULLY SHE KNEW TO MAKE ME RINSE MY MOUTH WITH MILK, THEN SPIT IT ALL OUT.

THERE HADN'T BEEN ENOUGH LYE TO BURN MY THROAT. I RECOVERED-- THOUGH MUCH ABASHED AT WHY I JUST PICKED UP A DIRTY SPOON TO PUT IN MY MOUTH, NOT KNOWING WHAT WAS ON IT. PERHAPS MIFFED AT DODIE TOO FOR NOT RINSING OFF THE SPOON. MY PARENTS DID NOT FIND OUT ABOUT THIS LITTLE SCARE UNTIL THE NEXT MORNING.

--SPRING, C. 1930

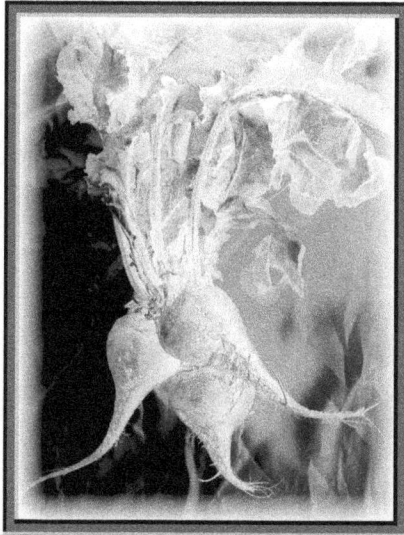

# CHAPTER 17:
## THE LAST SUPPER.

*"HERE'S YOUR HAT, THERE'S THE DOOR—*
*WHAT'S YOUR HURRY!"*

--DAD

J UST another ordinary weekday supper. What I would give for the opportunity to sit down with my family and sup with them one more time. I especially liked our winter meals-- hearty and filling, comfort food in the truest sense.

...When Mother awoke from her nap after making lunch for Homer, the Farm & Dairy she had been reading lay at her feet, blocking the register. She realized that is why her legs were cold.

She went over and tucked the quilt around Homer. He was *snooziling* noiselessly and she left him be. She quietly pulled the black wicker rocker back to its place next to Dad's rocker.

In the kitchen she moved silently. She took a pan down cellar to gather up some potatoes for supper. She paused to throw two shovelfuls of coal into the furnace. No one had been down there since morning. The firebox was hungry.

Bread pudding was on her mind for dessert. While in the fruit cellar, she filled the pan with a dozen baker-sized white potatoes then took down a quart jar of beef canned earlier in the year. Now Mother's hands were full.

Back in the kitchen, Mother sank into a chair at the table, prepared to pare her 10,000th potato without fanfare.

The peels went in the pig bucket under the sink. A pot filled with salted water stood standby on the stove as Mother stoked the fire for supper. With some time on her hands then, she tried to get ahead of her sewing. She laid out a pattern for an apron. A little more than an hour later, she donned a brand-new apron. By then it was ten minutes past five. Everyone had arrived home by that time. Mother was a bit late in getting supper going. Delmus was up at the barn doing the evening milking. Dad was up feeding the chickens. Doris was asked to set the table.

"It's Elaine's turn," Dodie said. "I did it *last* night."

"You did *not!*" Elaine said. "I did! Whadda dummy!"

"Big *liar!*" Dodie said. "I did and you <u>know</u> it!"

"You're the big, sneaky liar," Elaine retorted.

"That's it," Mother said. "You both do it."

That nipped that in the bud.

Meanwhile, I was busy chasing Homer around the living room, Dad's room and kitchen. I didn't chase him upstairs because it was too cold up there. (I must wonder what I did with Homer once I caught him, because I was always chasing him.)

Mother added kindling to the firebox in the stove to pick the fire back up. In a mixing bowl, she whipped together kitchen eggs, fresh milk, a dash of vanilla, a cup of white sugar, and sprinkled in cinnamon and nutmeg. She tore up stale bread into chunks and placed them in a tin baking pan. She poured the egg mixture over the bread, tossed in a handful of raisins at the last minute, stirred the bread pudding and placed it in the oven.

The stove was hot enough then. The potato water caught up to our 6-p.m. suppertime— as though trying to boil quickly to please Mother. The canned beef wound up in a cast-iron skillet. There was plenty of white, hard beef fat in the jar to simmer the meat without scorching it.

"Marcell," Mother said, "Stop chasing your little brother. Go down and getta jar of tomatoes."

I was too scared of the dark to head out on such a venture without reinforcements. Homer was too little for the mission—what good was he? Useless! Somebody had to go along to protect me from the spooks down there. Eerie.

"Elaine," I said, "come with me."

"I don't wanna."

"Mom, make Elaine come down with me."

"Scaredy-pants!"

"Am not," I said. "You're just a dumb bunny."

"You are!" Elaine said. "Why do you need help?"

"Carrying the tomatoes!" I was convinced my retort displayed sound logic.

"How are both of us going to carry ONE jar up the steps?" Elaine asked. "Dum-Dum!"

"That's enough," Mother said. "Doris, go with Marcell." Everyone in the room knows without saying that Mother has meted out justice for Doris's egregious act toward Elaine at breakfast that same morning (kicking Elaine under the table then staunchly denying it).

I trotted behind Dodie. Homer tagged along. We hit the bottom of the cellar steps and Mother called down.

"And bring up a jar of green beans and a pint of pickles," she said. "And DON'T run up the steps!"

We handed the pickles to Homer. Dodie and I looked at each other sideways.

Of course we ran up the steps.

At the landing, Homer tripped. The sound of the back door shutting announced Dad's arrival from the laying house. Gasp! The plot thickened. We froze. We stood there staring at each other, a trio of open mouths. When we realized Homer had not broken the pickle jar, and that Dad must have missed the commotion, we started to giggle. (When in doubt... giggle.) Then we noticed Homer had wet his pants. We were all scared of what Dad might have said (or done) had that jar broken, especially just after Mother's admonishment.

Mother and Elaine came to the landing to see what the clumping around and giggling was all about. They relieved us of the jars, Dodie helped as Homer relieved himself of his soiled knickers, I was relieved I didn't have to go down cellar alone and our little gang was relieved the jar hadn't busted open, especially with Dad afoot.

There was still much giggling going on when we sat down to eat. On the way to his seat, Delmus pulled my hair. I quit giggling and I was ready to cry and did. I quit crying long enough to ponder a way to get back at him.

Mother served the mashed potatoes. She was relieved the potatoes cooked thoroughly after a late start to supper. She had added milk to mash them, with a good portion of butter, salt and pepper. To the beef broth in the skillet, she added white flour. That made a rich, thick brown gravy to fill the center of a mound of mashed potatoes. Ah, yes!

---

"SIL VOUS PLAÎT," I SAID, SNOOTILY, "PASSÉ MOI LES TOMMES DE PERRE." I WAS SO PROUD OF MY SKILLS WITH FRENCH, ENGLISH AND OTHER FOREIGN LANGUAGES.

"YOU BIG DUMMY!" DODIE SAID, SETTING DOWN HER PLATE WITH A THUD. "IT'S 'POMMES DE TERRE' NOT 'TOMMES DE PERRE.' GEE."

"DORIS," MOTHER SAID, "IF MARCELL *WERE* A DUMMY, WHY DID MISS SMITH SKIP HER INTO THIRD GRADE?"

"BECAUSE," DELMUS SAID, "SHE WAS TEACHER'S PET?"

"DELMUS," DAD SAID, "I DON'T BELIEVE MOTHER WAS TALKIN' TO YOU."

"I THINK YOU MIGHT OWE MARCELL AN APOLOGY," MOTHER SAID.

"BUT SHE GOT ALL THE WORDS WRONG," DODIE SAID.

MOTHER SET HER FORK DOWN.

"'M SORRY," DODIE SAID. SHE GLARED AT ME ACROSS THE TABLE FOR A FEW SECONDS THROUGH SQUINTED EYESE.

"SHE DUH-UDN'T MEAN IT," I SAID, MUTTERING UNDER MY BREATH.

---

The braised beef was ladled onto our plates next to the potatoes. The tomatoes were served at room temperature in a bowl— probably the same bowl Flo put on our heads for those bowl haircuts. The bread-and-butter pickles sat on the table in the jar—we were not so fancy that we had to transfer them into a dish. Mother had warmed up the green beans and served them in a white bowl. Everything was white—the bowls, the walls and everything in-between.  (We didn't have any <u>colored</u> of anything except food.)  Sliced bread sat on a plate. Fresh butter was on the table too, in a dish.  This was a colorful dinner.  Red tomatoes, green beans, yellow butter, white potatoes, brown gravy.

Mother had left the oven door open a crack. She did not want dessert to burn.  I sat there toying with possible tricks I might pull on Delmus. I could smell the irresistible aroma of Mother's indescribable bread pudding issuing inevitably from the stove.

This typical supper might have taken place on any given Tuesday or Wednesday, with Mother already dreading the thought of the Stewarts showing up unannounced for yet another Sunday dinner...

**WE ALWAYS HOPED IT WAS THE <u>LAST</u> LAST SUPPER**
**BUT THEY SHOWED RIGHT UP AGAIN**
**THE VERY NEXT SUNDAY.**
**WE DIDN'T EVEN BOTHER RIDDING UP THE HOUSE FOR THEM.**

# VIGNETTE: THE PUNCH LINE.

*W*E HAD FREQUENT VISITORS FOR SUNDAY DINNER. THESE WERE THE STEWARTS. YES, MARTHA STEWART OF SUPER-DUM-DUM-LARCENY FAME AND HER EQUALLY-PRESUMPTUOUS PARENTS, JOHN AND ANNA. DAD AND JOHN WORKED AS CARPENTERS IN YOUNGSTOWN. THE STEWARTS CAME SUNDAY AFTER SUNDAY FOR MONTHS ON END AND GRACED US WITH THEIR PRESENCE— INVITED OR UN-- NEVER BROUGHT ALONG A JAR OF PICKLES OR A COVERED DISH OR EVEN A NICE CHERRY PIE FROM THE A&P FOR MOTHER.

ANNA STEWART MUST NOT HAVE BEEN A VERY GOOD COOK. THEY HAD SIX CHILDREN, SOME GROWN. THREE OR FOUR OF THESE STRUNG ALONG WHEN THEIR PARENTS "DROPPED BY." MOTHER'S SPECIALTY WAS FRIED CHICKEN. SHE WAS NOT FAMOUS FOR IT BUT IT WAS GOOD. UNDERSTATEMENT-- MORE THAN GOOD, IT WAS DELICIOUS. MOTHER PREPARED THREE WHOLE CHICKENS FOR SUNDAY DINNER. SHE SALTED THE CHICKEN AND FRIED IT WITH THE SKIN ON, RENDERING IT CRISPY, SALTY, CRUNCHY AND KIND OF BUBBLY. DELECTABLE. I LIKED THE DRUMSTICK BECAUSE IT WAS EASY TO HOLD. THE STEWARTS DROVE IN FROM YOUNGSTOWN 30 MILES AWAY BUT SOMEHOW ARRIVED EACH WEEK THE EXACT MOMENT DINNER WAS READY (AS PERFECTLY AS TALL MAN'S SUPPER APPEARANCE WAS TIMED). THEY ARRIVED AT THE STROKE OF NOON. QUITE UNCANNY. THEY DIDN'T NEED TO GO INTO THE LIVING ROOM TO SIT AND WAIT. THEY PLOPPED DOWN IN THE KITCHEN. IT WAS LIKE FAST FOOD. THE TABLE NEEDED AN EXTRA LEAF TO ACCOMMODATE THEM. OUR RANKS SWELLED IN EXCESS OF 14 PEOPLE AT THE TABLE.

"BLANCHE!" JOHN ANNOUNCED ONE SUNDAY TOWARD THE END OF DINNER. "YOU MAKE THE <u>BEST</u> FRIED CHICKEN!"

"WHY, THANK YOU, JOHN," MOTHER SAID. SHE BLUSHED. BEING THE SMART ALECK I WAS, I QUICKLY THOUGHT, "*CAR<u>NE</u> DIEM.*"

"YES!" I PIPED UP. "IF A CHICKEN DIES DURING THE WEEK, WE HAVE IT FOR SUNDAY DINNER!"

EVEN MOTHER COULDN'T STIFLE A GRATIFYING SMIRK. WE WOOLFS WATCHED IN GLEE AS THE STEWARTS (INCLUDING MARTHA) GOT A COMEUPPANCE. THESE FREELOADERS TURNED VARIOUS SHADES OF GREEN AT MY STOMACH-CHURNING ANNOUNCEMENT. HOWEVER...MY CHARADE DID NOT DERAIL THE STEWARTS FROM ROLLING IN THE NEXT SUNDAY... OR THE ONE AFTER THAT.

# A Limerick.

" **W**HEN A CHICKEN DIES DURING THE WEEK."

**W**HILE THOSE STEWARTS WERE FINGER LICKIN',

" **T**HERE WAS," I SAID, "WHO DIED-- ...A *CHICKEN*."

**T**HOUGH I LIED, JOHN WAS MORTIFIED,

**W**HILE MOTHER FRIED, ANNA CRIED.

**T**HOSE FREELOADERS I WAS HOPIN' ...TO SICKEN.

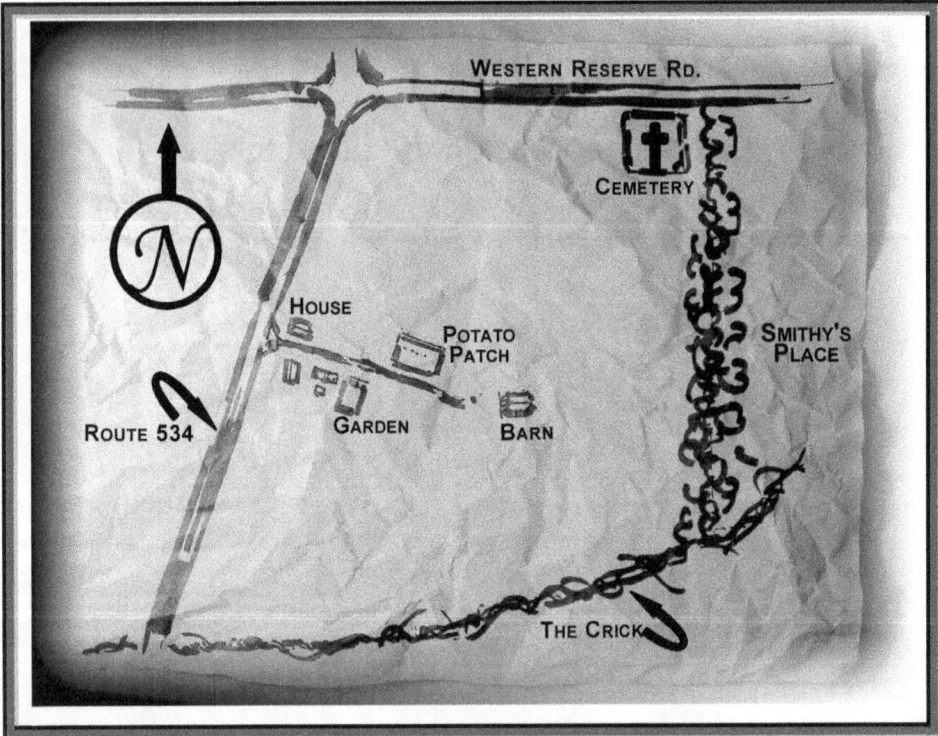

Figure 4: **WILLOW RUN FARM, 1930's.** ILLUSTRATION BY J. GRENGA.

# VIGNETTE: OTHER FAMOUS EVENTS OF 1924.

- JAN 25: 1ST WINTER OLYMPIC GAMES, CHAMONIX, FRANCE
- FEB 12: "RHAPSODY IN BLUE," NEW YORK DEBUT
- MAY 10: J. EDGAR HOOVER APPOINTED HEAD, FBI
- JUN 5: 1ST TRANSOCEANIC FACSIMILE TRANSMITTED
- JUL 14: BASTILLE DAY (MARCELLA WOOLF IS BORN)
- AUG 18: FRANCE WITHDRAWS TROOPS FROM GERMANY
- SEP: BELGIUM STARTS THE EIGHT-HOUR WORKDAY
- OCT 22: TOASTMASTERS FOUNDED
- NOV 4: 1ST FEMALE U.S. GOVERNOR ELECTED (WYOMING)
- NOV 29: PUCCINI, ITALIAN OPERETTIST, DIES
- DEC 24: CROYDON AIR FIELD CRASH LEAVES EIGHT DEAD

## 1924 BIRTHS:
- JEAN-FRANCOIS REVEL, MARGARET TRUMAN, GLORIA VANDERBILT, HANK STRAM, SARAH VAUGHAN, MARLON BRANDO, DORIS DAY, HENRY MANCINI, SIR NEVILLE MARRINER, TOM LANDRY, AUDIE MURPHY, EVA MARIE SAINT, BUDDY HACKETT, DON KNOTTS, CARROLL O'CONNOR, ROD SERLING, ED KOCH, JEANETTE SCHMID, TRUMAN CAPOTE, JIMMIE CARTER, ROSAMUNDE PILCHER, ANNETTE STRAUS

## 1924 DEATHS:
- WOODROW WILSON, JOSEPH CONRAD, FRANZ KAFKA, VICTOR HERBERT, VLADIMIR LENIN

# ABOUT THE AUTHORS.

MARCELLA WOOLF GRENGA— WAS BORN in 1924 on a farm in Berlin Center, Ohio. By grit and wit, the Woolf family survived the Great Depression intact. Along with five siblings, Marcella began her formal education in a one-room school. In 1942, Marcella entered nurses training and served as a cadet nurse (eligible to join the Army or Navy Nurse Corps), as an Emergency Room Head Nurse, and as a nurse administrator. She and her husband, Edward, raised five children and owned a machine and welding business more than 30 years. An entrepreneur and artist, Marcella operated a stained-glass shop. Marcella completed seven World Cruises aboard the ocean liner, Queen Elizabeth 2, traveling from east to west (from west to east...?). Marcella is currently writing the second volume of the Willow Run Farm trilogy.

JODY LaRaine GRENGA— WAS BORN in 1956 in Youngstown, Ohio. Twice alumna of The Ohio State University, she earned a doctorate degree in chiropractic in 1991. With nearly 13 years enlisted service, Dr. Grenga retired as a captain from the Texas Army National Guard as a decorated Medical Service Corps officer. She served military tours in Germany, Guatemala and Panama and has published more than 40 articles, book reviews, cartoons and one book. "The Writings of Florence Scovel Shinn" was republished to include an illustrated biography of Mrs. Shinn based on Dr. Grenga's research. Her first book, "Sales Force," was published in 2007. Dr. Grenga is currently writing a book about rainwater purification.

www.ingramcontent.com/pod-product-compliance
Lightning Source LLC
Chambersburg PA
CBHW020243290326
41930CB00038B/197